FINANCIAL
PLANNING

FINANCIAL
PLANNING

Dr. Apsara
Dr. Srinath
Shwetha K R
Vignesh K
Dr. S. Rani

FINANCIAL PLANNING

by: Dr. Apsara, Dr. Srinath, Shwetha K R, Vignesh K, Dr. S. Rani

■

RED'SHINE PUBLICATION PVT. LTD.

Headquarters (India): 88-90 REDMAC, Navamuvada,
Lunawada, India-389 230
Contact: +91 76988 26988
Registration no. GJ31D0000034

In Association with,

RED'MAC INTERNATIONAL PRESS & MEDIA. INC

India | Sweden | UK

■

■

■

ISBN: 978-93-93239-70-9
ISBN-10: 93-93239-70-3
DIP: 18.10.9393239703
DOI: 10.25215/9393239703
Price: ₹ 400
January, 2022 (First Edition)

■

■

www.redshine.co.in | info@redshine.in
Printed in India | Title ID: 9393239703

CONTENTS

MODULE-1

INTRODUCTION

Some of the things in life that you plan for and others that you don't are constantly in competition with each other. You may already have a general idea of what you want to accomplish that requires money. For example, the purchase of a home and having children, as well as paying for their educations and marriages. A broken-down automobile or hospital bill can put a burden on anyone's finances, regardless of their financial situation. With a financial plan in place, you can develop yourself no matter what life throws at you — by savings and investing in financial vehicles which are specifically tailored to your goals. To avoid being taken by surprise by life's twists and turns, it's a good idea to consult a financial counsellor. Having a financial advisor can help you keep up with changes in the financial markets, laws of Tax and the economy. The ups and downs of life can be difficult to navigate without the guidance of a financial counselor you can rely on and a financial plan you develop together.

DEFINITION OF FINANCIAL PLANNING

Different authors have different opinions about financial planning. These views can be classified into two parts:

(1) Narrow Concept of Financial Planning: According to this view, in financial planning, it is estimated how much capital is required for business. According to some other authors, financial planning means capital structure. Thus, according to those who hold this view, financial planning is the process which predict the company's assets ,needs and the design of its capital structure. *"Financial Plan is the act of deciding in advance the quantum of capital requirements and its forms."* – **R.M. Shrivastava**

(2) Broader Concept of Financial Planning: In a broad-sense, financial planning includes determination of financial goals, formulation of financial policies and development of financial procedures.

According to Arthur S. Dewing, the following activities are included in financial planning:

(i) Capitalisation i.e., determining the required amount of Capital;

(ii) Capital structure, i.e., deciding the various sources of capital and determining the mutual proportion of various securities;

(iii) Proper management of capital, i.e., managing the various types of assets.

Although the above concept of financial planning propounded by Dewing is quite comprehensive and reasonable, yet it fails to highlight upon its nature and functional areas more clearly. The definition given by **Walker, E.W. and Baughn, W.H**. seems to be more proper and appealing. According to them, "Financial Planning pertains only to the function of finance and includes the determination of the firm's financial objectives, financial policies and financial procedures."

Estimating the amount of money needed and gauging the level of competition is part of financial planning. An organization's procurement, investment, and fund management policies are formulated through this procedure.

You can achieve your life's goals by managing your finances effectively. Goals in life include buying a house and preparing for your child's.

Financial planning is the process of establishing how company can meet its strategic goals and objectives while keeping its costs in check. Each activity, resource, equipment and material needed to accomplish these objectives is detailed in the Financial Plan.

OBJECTIVES OF FINANCIAL PLANNING

Financial Planning has got many objectives to look forward to:

a. **Determining capital requirements** There are many elements that will influence this, including the cost of current and fixed assets, the cost of advertising, and long-term planning It's important to consider both short-term and long-term capital needs.

b. **Determining capital structure**- In the context of a business, a company's capital structure refers to the type and amount of capital it needs, as well as its overall composition. Debt-equity ratio decisions, both short-term and long-term, are included here.

Finance managers ensure that the company's limited financial resources are utilized to their fullest potential at the lowest possible cost by defining financial policies in terms of cash management, lending, borrowing, and so on.

TYPES OF FINANCIAL PLANNING

On the basis of time, the process of financial planning may be of three types:

1. **Short-term Financial Planning:**

The financial plans drafted for a year or less in any business is called short-term financial planning. Such plans are prepared for the efficient use of working capital. The main objective of such planning is to maintain liquidity of business. Various types of short-term budget particularly cash budget, sales budget, production budget etc. and projected balance sheet, cash flow statement etc. are considered as the important tools of short-term planning.

2. **Medium-term Financial Planning**:

The plans prepared for more than one year but less than five years are called medium-term financial plans. Such planning is needed for meeting the needs for the maintenance of assets, assets replacement, Conducting Research and Development activities and arrangement of special working capital.

3. **Long-term Financial Planning**:

The planning which is done for more than 5 years is known as the long-term financial planning. This is done to get rid of the long-term financial problems of the organisation.

IMPORTANCE OF FINANCIAL PLANNING

Financing Planning is the course of mounting a company's strategy for managing its monetary resources in order to achieve its long-term financial goals. This guarantees that financial and investment policies are effective and adequate. The significance of financial planning can be summarised as: It gives a framework for making sound financial decisions. Each financial decision that you make has an impact on other parts of your finances. As an example, purchasing a specific financial product may help you pay off your mortgage faster, but it may also delay your retirement by a considerable amount of time. You can better understand the long-term and short-term impacts of your financial decisions by looking at them as part of a larger picture.

Financial planning is the most often requested questions.

1. There must be sufficient finances available.
2. Maintaining a steady flow of money is possible with the help of financial planning.
3. Investors who want to put their money to good use can do so with confidence if a company practises sound financial planning.
4. Helps in the long-term viability of the organisation by formulating growth and expansion plans.
5. As a result of financial planning, there are less uncertainty when it comes to altering market patterns.

As a result of financial planning, the company's growth can be slowed down by lowering the risk of unexpected events. This ensures the company's long-term viability and profitability.

FINANCE FUNCTIONS

The following are the finance function

Investment Decision

The allocation of money to long-term assets is one of the most critical activities of finance. The term "capital budgeting" is used to describe this process. Investing in long-term assets is essential to maximising future returns. Investing involves the following two considerations:

Both new and existing investments are evaluated in terms of profitability and the cutoff rate is compared.

A return on investment can't be predicted because of a hazy future. Risk is associated with uncertainty, which must be taken into account. Investment returns might be significantly impacted by this risk factor. For an investment idea to succeed, it is essential to consider both the expected return and risk.

Long-term asset allocation is not the sole consideration when making investment decisions. Rather, the decision also entails deciding how to use the proceeds from the sale of assets that are no longer profitable or productive

In order to determine the opportunity cost of capital, it is necessary to dissolve these assets. The opportunity cost of the needed rate of return is used to calculate the relevant cut-off rate (RRR).

Financial Decision

Making financial decisions is also part of the job of a financial manager. A company's ability to operate effectively depends on how, when, and where it gets its money. There are numerous ways to raise money. As a general rule, a healthy equity to debt ratio is required. It is the company's combination of stock and debt funding that is referred to as its capital structure.

A company's stock rises in value, and so does its stockholders' wealth. This is a win-win situation. A shareholder's risk and return can be affected by debt, on the other hand. It's a little more risky, but it could increase stock investment returns..

In the eyes of many, a solid financial structure is one that seeks to maximise shareholder value while minimising risk. There would be an optimal capital structure as a result of the company's increased market value. When deciding a company's capital structure, there are a number of other tools that can be used.

Dividend Decision

The goal of all businesses is to make a profit or a favourable return on their investment. However, the main responsibility of a financial manager is to determine whether to distribute all profits to shareholders, keep a portion of them and distribute the rest to the firm, or distribute a portion of the profits to shareholders and keep the rest for the business.

The finance manager is accountable for formative the best dividend policy for the company in order to make the most of its market value. therefore, the optimal dividend payout ratio can be determined. In the event of a company's success, it is normal practise to pay regular dividends to shareholders.

Liquidity Decision

To avoid bankruptcy, a company must have a strong liquidity position. When a company invests in current assets, its profitability, liquidity, and risk are all affected. There must be enough money invested in current assets in order to maintain the balance between profitability and liquidity. When it comes to investing in current assets, it's significant to remain in mind that they don't pay any dividends to the company.

A company's current assets should be accurately appraised and then disposed of when they are no longer profitable, if necessary. Use current assets in times of financial distress and bankruptcy.

FINANCIAL PLANNING PROCESS

Managing a person's financial affairs in an integrated and coordinated manner is what financial planning is all about. You should utilise your financial plan as a roadmap throughout your life rather than a binder that sits on your bookshelf gathering dust.

In the financial planning process, there are six distinct stages that can be identified:

Step 1: Establishing and Defining the Client-Planner Relationship

Establishing and Defining the Relationship between the Client and the Planner

First, we need to establish a common ground with our financial planning clients. We'll have to work together to figure out what has to be done and what the terms, criteria, and limitations are. This is a two-way street.

Step 2: Gathering Client Data, including Goals

We must first acquire information about our clients and their aims before we can examine any plan. The client's objectives govern every step of the financial planning process. During this stage, we collect information such as:

- Data in the form of numbers
- Intangibles and monetary obligations
- The incoming and outgoing flow of financial resources
- Replicas of trusts and wills
- A breakdown of recent investment activity
- Information on employee benefits and retirement plans Expenses
- Family tree in broad strokes
- Information on any businesses owned or operated by customers
- Details about a policy of insurance
- Financial advisors' names, addresses, and phone numbers
- Retirement benefits are offered.
- The last three years of tax returns

- The Qualitative Data
- Life-altering changes that may occur in the future
- Expectations and goals for the workplace (dreams and desires)
- Client and family members' well-being (heredity issues as well)
- What you like to do in your spare time
- Assumptions in the planning process
- How much you're willing to risk

The step of acquiring data is critical since it is impossible to make well-informed decisions without correct data.

Step 3: Analyzing and Evaluating the Client's Financial Status

The financial planner conducts a thorough evaluation of all pertinent data and papers at this stage. With the support of other professionals in the fields of tax and estate planning, he or she develops strategies and recommendations to help the client achieve their objectives.

Step 4: Developing and Presenting Financial Planning Recommendations/Alternatives

Before a financial strategy is finalised, we meet with customers to go over the recommendations, possibilities, and alternatives. We seek the advice of other experts in fields in which we lack the necessary training or experience. For extensive tax guidance, for example, we would utilise a qualified attorney or a qualified CPA

Step 5: Implementing the Financial Planning Recommendations

it's time to put the financial planning recommendations into action

The financial planner and the customer work together to implement the strategy. Financial strategies have little significance unless they are implemented.

Step 6: monitoring the Financial Planning Recommendations

It is impossible to know if the clients' goals are being reached or if progress is being achieved

Without. As a guide, map or manual, the financial plan is not designed to be looked at once and put aside.

TIPS FOR MAKING THE MOST OF THE FINANCIAL PLANNING PROCESS

1. Start right away. No matter how old you are, starting today is always preferable to dithering for another five years. Every day is important.
2. be completely open and truthful with you. look for assistance if you require it.
3. Set goals that are attainable and measurable. Don't put too much stock on the outcomes of your financial planning.
4. Continually review your financial condition and plan, and make adjustments as necessary.
5. You should always keep an eye on the performance of your investments and take money out if you need to.
6. Get your hands dirty. No one else is going to do your work for you, because it's your money and your responsibility.

THE CLIENT-PLANNER RELATIONSHIP: INTRODUCING YOURSELVES

Establish and define the client-planner relationship. This first step allows you as the financial planner to sit the client down and discuss the services that are being offered. For example, explain to your client your history with financial planning and how your background will help you reach their financial goals.

As individuals we all want our money to last, but how do we do this? As planners, we can help others achieve their goals by establishing a strong client-planner relationship.

When building this relationship, the client must identify themselves to you, the planner. It is important that you as the planner knows who you are working with. Meaning is you working with an individual, a family, or a business/organization.

As the financial planner, you should then tell your client(s) about your qualifications, expertise and methodology of financial planning. This will help your client gain find comfort in this new relationship you are building with them. Communication is a key element in order for this relationship to be effective.

An open and honest connection is essential to achieving those objectives. The relationship between a client and a financial advisor is more than just statistics, and it can be extremely personal. In order to be successful in the work you do together, you need to have a good relationship with your advisor It has been established that trust between financial planners ;

The relationship between an advisor and a client appears to be built on a foundation of trust. A financial advisor's ability to build and keep a client's trust is just as important as his or her knowledge of the financial markets.

By working with an experienced financial planning expert, a client can determine whether or not that professional's services and competencies are appropriate for their situation. There are many factors that a financial planner must take into consideration when assessing his or her capacity to meet the needs of a customer. In the event of a conflict of interest, a financial planner will declare it.

An agreement between the financial planner and the client is reached.

As part of a written engagement agreement, a financial planning professional lays out in full all of the parties' responsibilities, as well as their pay and conflicts of interest.

Documents signed by both parties or formally acknowledged by the client outline the scope of the engagement, which includes a method for ending the contract.

KEY STRATEGIES TO BUILD CLIENT RELATIONSHIPS FOR FINANCIAL PLANNERS

Discovery. In the art of selling and building new professional relationships, the ability to ask the appropriate questions is essential. To help your customer uncover flaws or gaps in their plans, you should have a good conversation with them first. Conversations are sparked by open-ended inquiries, which require less talking and more listening. Relationships can be built on trust and solid foundations in face-to-face meetings. While it's important to meet face-to-face with your prospects and clients, it's widely accepted that this isn't always possible in today's globe.

When it comes to connecting with your clients truly, the effort you put forth will go a long way in this case, too.

The Information-Gathering Stage.

In order to get to know your client better, you'll need to get some basic personal and financial information about them, such as their name, address, and phone number. It's critical to get both the concrete facts and the fuzzy rationale that go into a client's goals. Client information must be protected and the customer experience must be excellent by using technology. We spend a lot of effort and money to ensure that sensitive information is transferred and stored securely. Understanding the client's goals and ensuring that their sensitive information is protected are both critical components of this step.

Validating the Data. As soon as you've gathered data from your client, it's time to do some analysis on it. When it comes to interpreting hard data, it's important to keep in mind the client's perspective, which is captured in soft data. Keep in mind, hard statistics may not always agree with their account of their circumstance. An illustration of this is when a customer claims to have complete faith in their life insurance policy, but the numbers reveal otherwise. Or vice versa - the customer may feel that based on their growth in spending and extension of their family that they need to change their life insurance programme, when in fact this was addressed initially with their original plan design. To acquire your clients' trust and establish your reputation, look for areas where you can fill in the holes they've identified, so that they may get back on track to the retirement they'd envisioned.

Strategic Solutions and Implementation In this step, you'll provide the solutions you came up with based on the client's facts and goals. Seeing the flaws in their current strategy as an opportunity can help people recognise their financial goals rather than the labour it will take to achieve them. The best way to help your client through the estate planning process is to help them imagine what their future will look like. It's time to set together a team to implement the strategy once the client has given you the go-ahead. As the quarterback, you coordinate the efforts of their accountants, attorneys, and financial advisers to ensure that the strategy is carried out as intended. To ensure that the consumer feels supported throughout the entire process, it's critical that your team members share your values.

Ongoing Client Service. Consider the long-term viability of your relationship with a client after you've done business with them. Why do people put their faith in you and your organisation to help them achieve their dreams? There is still a lot of work to be done. You need to show your clientele how important they are to your business. Having the right people on your team, communicating effectively, and staying creative are all essential components of this process. Your client will interact with multiple members of your team on a regular basis in order to maintain their account running well. It's up to you to ensure that the second time around is as as enjoyable as the first time around. There's a fine line between attracting new clients and keeping them for the long run. Their long-term goals may be influenced by changes in their personal lives. Don't wait for things to go wrong before you take action. Let your customers know that you are open to new ideas and that they should come to you with any changes they are experiencing by presenting them to them. The foundation you built with them will be tested as you continue to serve them throughout their lifetimes. If you treat them like a member of the family, they will treat you the same.

Every interaction with a client should emphasise the importance of the relationship. In my opinion, we don't talk enough about the importance of striking a balance between being a human being and running a business. It is my hope that my storey can serve as a guide for anyone in need, and that we can continue to move forward together by examining the changes that we are currently experiencing.

FINANCIAL PLANNING CONCEPTS

DIVERSIFICATION

By diversifying your investments, you may be able to mitigate some of the risks you face. The importance of diversity is often emphasized by events in the financial markets, such as stock price drops. When the economy changes, each investment type reacts differently.

A decline in one asset could be compensated by an increase or stability in another if you have a varied portfolio. It is important to remember, however, that diversification does not guarantee success or protect against the risk of losing money. As a result, it might assist you in reaching your financial objectives.

ASSET ALLOCATION

Asset allocation is a long-term approach aimed to assist investors accomplish their financial goals without accepting unnecessary risk. There are many distinct sorts of investments, and because of this, they typically react to changes in the economy and financial markets in different ways.

Stocks, which carry a higher level of risk, can be included in a long-term financial plan, but their value can fluctuate, putting your portfolio at greater danger. Fixed income investments, on the other hand, are considered less risky, but the returns can be more conservative. Public utility stocks, preferred equities and federally tax-free1 municipal bonds all have the advantage of monthly interest or dividend payments, but the increase on your initial investment is much smaller. Asset allocation does not guarantee a profit or protect against a loss, though. Be sure to discuss all of your assets with your financial advisor while putting together a financial strategy, including those in other accounts, real estate, collectibles, and so on. To ensure that your overall asset allocation is in line with your goals and risk tolerance, this is the step to take.

TIME HORIZON

If you have more time on your hands, you'll be more willing to take on more risk. Those who are just starting out in their careers, for example, may have a greater window of opportunity to take advantage of the wealth-building power of compounding.

Because of the longer time horizon available to counterbalance any losses, this person may be ready to take on more investing risk in exchange for the potential for bigger profits. In contrast, less risky assets are usually preferred by those who are nearing the end of their careers and are preparing for retirement. It is possible that this person has a larger reserve fund and is more concerned with protecting their possessions than increasing their wealth. You need to make adjustments to your asset allocation strategy as you move through different stages of life.

TAX PLANNING

After allocating your assets, you must decide whether to invest them in a tax-deferred or taxable account. After all, it's what's left over after taxes that counts these days. Taxable accounts, like a stock portfolio, are where you deposit money that has already been taxed. You can contribute to a tax-deferred account by using monies that have not been taxed yet. Your money can grow faster in tax-deferred accounts because you don't have to pay annual taxes on donations or capital gains. Because of this, it is important to be aware that any funds that you withdraw from the account are subject to taxation. Because you are more likely to be in a lower tax rate when you retire, tax-deferred accounts are perfect for retirement savings investments.

When you take the money out of the bank. There are ways to reduce your tax burden even in a taxable account, as long as you know how. An index fund that tracks the S&P 500 is likely to have lower turnover than an actively managed fund with more stock turnover. Ordinary income taxes are levied on interest payments on bonds, which typically disperse a significant portion each year.

CHOOSING A FINANCIAL ADVISOR

When it comes to picking a financial advisor, it's as personal as choosing a physician. While it may seem counterintuitive to talk about one's finances in this way, it is also an excellent approach to reveal one's priorities and values. It's important to trust your advisor with sensitive information that you may not be able to share with friends or family. Your financial advisor should also be trusted because it's essential that you feel comfortable adopting their advice - something you may not do with your family and friends. When interviewing a potential advisor, it's important to find out how he or she is compensated for the time they spend with you.

It is not uncommon for financial planners to charge a fixed annual or hourly payment for their services (wherein you pay a fixed annual fee or hourly rate). Additionally, financial advisors are paid a percentage of a client's assets under their care, as well as commissions on certain transactions.

THE RISK PLANNING SPECTRUM

Generally, the rule of thumb is that the more the risk assumed, the bigger the possible return on that investment. To reduce portfolio risk while also increasing possible rewards, diversification investments across a range of asset classes can be an effective strategy.

ISSUES AND ANALYSIS CHALLENGES IN FINANCIAL PLANNING PROCESS

The most challenging component of building a sustainable financial plan simply understands how much they are currently spending, and, by extension, being able to accurately predict what it's going to cost to fund the lifestyle they want in retirement. Financial planning is a necessary for every finance department and for any organisation that wishes to be in financial control. Unfortunately it is a tough task that is often inefficient and counterproductive. Budgeting and planning activities involve analytical and people skills, experience, and the support of technology to make it effective. To be effective, those responsible for financial planning must have knowledge into cost and revenue drivers, and be able to link their activities to the wider corporate business strategy.

Lack of Integrated Planning Tools —

Although sophisticated technological solutions exist for budgeting and planning, many firms are still running on Excel. Incorporating data from multiple sources using spreadsheets, on the other hand, is a waste of time. A spreadsheet's limited data management capabilities make it difficult to test several possibilities. Planners spend their time trying to integrate spreadsheets together or analyse difficulties that crop up within their spreadsheets.

Inefficient Processes –

If you do decide to fix your financial planning process, it’s crucial to identify exactly what you’re aiming to accomplish: Get planning closer to your business strategy?

Work with business units and departments to introduce drivers?

Accomplish improved variance reporting and analytics?

Produce corporate roll-up of plan and what-if scenarios?

Unclear business purpose and alignment

As if there weren't enough challenges enough, planners are often so agitated they ask themselves and their team, "Why are we doing this?" Many organisations have not built a culture where responsibility and openness are expected. This weakens the work of financial planning teams whose reports may in turn affect the outcome of variable compensation.

Data –

The ruler of the castle is the data. Weak data management makes simple activities such as obtaining real or forecast scenarios extremely difficult. There is no guarantee that the data you obtain will be accurate once you have obtained it, therefore concentrating on the data is essential.

Lack of Real-Time Information

Finance teams are under constant pressure to provide actionable insights to help decision making for business leaders who need up-to-the-minute information. Your financial planning system's level of detail is hampered by the absence of precise, real-time data.

Using this information, you may build a plan for your company's future. Self-service analytics features allow real-time information, helping you to identify which revenue streams are underperforming, how to enhance operational efficiencies, examine your company's performance, and establish an achievable plan for driving development. You can also update your plans as you go with any changes in the real-time information.

Lack of Collaboration

As with any business transformation effort, FP&A is doomed to failure if departments fail to work together effectively. Better visibility and more accurate forecasts are made possible by FP&A collaboration across all of your company's departments.

For instance, a system of shared information throughout the operations team helps with financial planning and cost minimization. Collaborative forecasting enables firms to transition away from disjointed and isolated forecasting operations to a single, real-time enterprise forecasting methodology.

Inaccurate Budgeting and Forecasting

Cloud-based financial forecasting systems can be very helpful in collecting and evaluating data, running scenarios, analysing techniques and prospective outcomes.

But, just having the appropriate solution isn't enough for effective financial forecasting. More commonly, the financial procedures are unreliable and need to be repaired, due to which the forecasts are wrong. Consistency in systems and processes is often lacking, which makes it difficult to make sound decisions.

Manual Tasks Take Too Much Time

Manual tasks such as account reconciliation and financial closing take up much too much of the time of finance experts. It is still difficult for many finance departments to cut their cycle time in half. Strategic tasks like FP&A are vital to create timely, useful insights. However, finance teams are spending most of their time sorting and organising data instead of evaluating it.

Disconnected Systems and Processes

The accuracy and timeliness of data from other sections of the company is critical to 77% of planning activities, according to Ventana Research. Therefore, combining the multiple planning stages brings several benefits. However, integrating plans from diverse sections of the business can be tough, especially if you are dealing with a number of disconnected spreadsheets. Cloud-based technologies make it easy to migrate from spreadsheets and link financial planning and analysis with other parts of the organisation.

Lack of Business Insights

A frequent difficulty encountered by most CFOs today is the low quality of data accessible and the inability to translate their business data into important insights. Spreadsheets are used by a large number of people and teams, and as a result, multiple versions of the same spreadsheet may exist, each with their own set of modifications, making it challenging to represent accurately.

Without a single source of truth, digging down and combining all the essential data is a long, manual and error-prone effort. Spreadsheets cannot accommodate an endless amount of calculations and macros which can leave your expanding firm without trustworthy models and predictions to make accurate budgets and forecasts. Senior management is unable to delve deeply into corporate data to uncover information that can be used to make informed decisions.

DOCUMENTATION REQUIRED FOR FINANCIAL PROCESSES

Entrepreneurs spend a lot of time and energy on day-to-day operations like customer service, sales, and inventory management when they are just starting out.

Having a thorough understanding of your company's financials is just as important to long-term growth and success.

For business owners, these are the five most important financial records they need to keep track of. Using all of these financial data together provides an accurate picture of your company's health.

Here's why these five financial documents are vital to small businesses.

The five important documents include profit and loss statements, balance sheets, cash-flow statements, tax returns and ageing reports. They help you ask the proper questions and find answers that are particular to your firm, such as: \sWhether your business revenue flows continuously or your sales and services are more cyclical.

If your company is making money, barely breaking even, or even losing money, you're doing something right.

Which commodities and services create the most profit and which are loss leaders.

These materials can help you establish effective, data-driven strategies for everything from personnel and inventory management to adding sites or minimising losses. They assist you see if, how and when it's sensible to invest in new equipment or take out a loan to cover tighter periods. If you're looking for cash, partners, or investors, you'll be better off with their assistance.

Even better, you can get these records through your company's accounting software or from your bookkeeper or CPA (CPA).

1. Profit and loss (P&L) statement

A profit and loss (P&L) statement, commonly referred to as an income statement, is used to evaluate current financial position and potential for growth. A P&L describes business revenues generated and expenses incurred during a given period of time. Whatever's left after the expenses are eliminated is profit, and if expenses exceed sales, then your P&L indicates a loss.

Profit and Loss Statement Template

[Company Name]

[Street Address], [City, ST ZIP Code]
[Phone: 555-555-55555] [Fax: 123-123-123456]
[abc@example.com]

Profit & Loss Statement

For the Period Ended ________________

Income	**$**	**$**
Sales	0000000	
Services	00000000	
Other Income	00000	
Total Income		**0000000**
Expenses		
Accounting	0000000	
Advertising	000000	
Assets Small	000000	
Bank Charges	000000	
Cost of Goods Sold	00000	
Total Expenses		**00000000**
Profit/Loss		**00000000**

Only the revenue or expenses related to the current year are debited or credited to profit and loss account. The profit and loss account starts with **gross profit at the credit side** and if there is a gross loss, it is shown on the debit side.

Many small businesses suffer losses from time to time, especially when starting out or expanding. A "red flag" for business owners is a persistent loss since it indicates that more money is being spent than being earned. When you keep a close eye on your finances, you'll be able to catch these problems before they get out of hand.

2. Cash flow statement

An often-quoted figure highlights the necessity of maintaining healthy cash flow: 82 percent of the small firms that fail do so because of cash flow concerns. Regularly checking your cash flow statement can go a long way in assisting your organisation to stay on the plus side of that number.

While a P&L merely displays money in and money out for a certain time, the cash flow statement is more like a budget, used to estimate revenue in and expenses out over a time period - commonly, approximately three years. In order for your business to run smoothly, you must pay both fixed and variable expenses out of the revenue your company earns (in addition to bank loans, taxes and the purchases of new assets, if needed). A company's ability to meet these obligations is demonstrated in the cash flow statement.

Having a clear picture of a company's cash flow is important for all stakeholders, including owners, lenders, and investors.

A cash flow statement (CFS) is a key indication of strength, profitability, and the long-term future prognosis of a company. Using the CFS, you can figure out whether or not a business has enough liquid assets to cover its bills. A CFS can assist a business forecast its future cash flow, which is helpful for planning purposes.

Cash flow statement for XYZ business for the year ended 31st of December 2020	
	$
CASH FLOW FROM OPERATING ACTIVITIES	
Cash receipts from customers	83,000
Cash paid to suppliers	(25,000)
Cash paid to employees	(23,000)
Cash paid for other operating expenses	(8,000)
Cash generated from operations	27,000
Dividends received*	250
Interest received	500
Interest paid	(500)
Tax paid	(2,450)
Net cash flow from operating activities	24,800
CASH FLOW FROM INVESTING ACTIVITIES	
Additions to equipment	(2,500)
Replacement of equipment	(7,000)
Proceeds** from sale of equipment	500
Net cash flow from investing activities	(9,000)
CASH FLOW FROM FINANCING ACTIVITIES	
Proceeds from capital contributed	3,400
Proceeds from loan	16,000
Payment of loan	(5,400)
Net cash flow from financing activities	14,000
NET INCREASE/DECREASE IN CASH	29,800
Cash at the beginning of the period	2,430
Cash at the end of the period	32,230

3. Balance sheet

You can keep tabs on the progress of your company's finances with the help of its balance sheet.

A company's quarterly or annual balance sheet, like its profit and loss statement (P&L), provides insight into how well a company is performing. Unlike P&Ls, though, your balance sheet provides a snapshot computation of your organization's assets, stated as business liabilities plus owner ownership.

Company Name Here

Balance Sheet

For the Period Ended ____________

Assets				Liabilities			
Current Assets				**Current Liabilities**			
Cash		XXXXXX		Accounts Payable		XXXXXX	
Short-Term Investments		XXXXX		Salaries Payable		XXXXX	
Accounts Receivables		XXXXX		Accrued Interest		XXXXX	
Inventories		XXXXXXX		Taxes Payable		XXXX	
Prepaid Insurance		XXXXXX		Current Portion of Notes		XXXXXX	XXXXXXXX
Others		XXXXX	XXXXXX				
Long-Term Investments				Long-Term Liabilities			
Stock Investments		XXXXXX		Note Payable		XXXXXX	
Cash Value of Investments		XXXXXXX	XXXXXX	Mortgage Liability		XXXXXX	XXXXXXXX
Fixed Assets				**Total Liabilities**			XXXXXXXX
Land		XXXXXX					
Building and Equipment	XXXXXXX			**Stock Holder's Equity**			
Less Accumulated Depreciation	(XXXXX)	XXXXXX	XXXXXXX	Capital Stock		XXXXXXXX	
				Retained Earnings		XXXXXXX	
Intangible Assets							
Good will			XXXXXXX	**Total Stock Holder's Equity**			XXXXXX
Other Assets							
Receivables from Employees			XXXXXXXX				
Total Assets			XXXXXXXXX	**Total Liabilities**			XXXXXXXXX

Short-term assets, such as cash in the company's checking account and goods, can be included in the list of available assets. Real estate and heavy machinery are examples of long-term assets. For a company's obligations, short-term debts like production costs and short-term loans are combined to form the total amount owed.

Equity involves capital invested by the owner or investors and retained earnings.

4. Tax returns

Most business owners are familiar with tax returns before they even open enterprises, because they've filed them as individuals. When you manage a business, it's vital to keep up with your business taxes, as well as any personal taxes that you may be liable for separately.

According to your company's corporate type and the tax repercussions that apply, you will need to fill out a specific tax form. Often, businesses utilise CPAs or other tax professionals to submit their taxes. It's crucial that you analyse yours, because it can help you and your financial team creates growth ideas that can be profitable to your organisation. When to hire new employees, purchase new equipment, or expand to new sites are just a few examples.

5. Accounts receivable/accounts payable (aka, "aging reports")

Debts due to a corporation are classified according to their age in an ageing report. "Accounts receivable" is the accounting word for funds that are owed to your firm, whereas "accounts payable" are the monies that your business owes to others. In business, it's commonly considered that the older a debt is, the smaller the possibility that it will be paid. If a business doesn't get paid, it loses money and can have an unhealthy cash flow.

Aging reports allow you identify how many accounts receivable are overdue and how old they are, so that you may follow up and take action to bring money in. Conversely, if you have invoices that are overdue, this should signify that you need to get caught up. Talk to your CPA and financial staff about how to better control spending and streamline processes.

FINANCIAL STATEMENT DISCLOSURE

Participants in a transaction receive a disclosure statement, which is a financial document outlining important details in clear language. Disclosure statements for retirement plans must clearly lay out who contributes to the plan, contribution limits, penalties, and tax status.

Financial statement disclosures provide internal and external business stakeholders with more information regarding a company's financial activities. Larger company organisations often utilise disclosures to convey additional information to lenders and investors.

It includes the name of the company, the party of the loans, permission, date, and place at which the document was signed, significant terms such as tenure of the loan, interest charged, annual percentage rate, total processing fees, loan statement, prepayment.

Accountants' assumptions in compiling a company's income statement, balance sheet, statement of changes in financial position, or statement of retained earnings are made explicit in the financial statements. The notes are necessary to completely comprehending these publications.

The disclosures can be mandatory by generally accepted accounting standards or elective per management decisions. Types of disclosures include, accounting changes, accounting errors, asset retirement, insurance contract amendments, and significant occurrences.

Purpose of Disclosures

Even if the financial statements of a corporation contain all of the pertinent financial data, this data typically requires more explanation. That is where the disclosures on the financial statement come into play.

A company's stakeholders will receive important information not included in the financial statement itself if the company makes a financial statement disclosure. The disclosures can be mandatory by generally accepted accounting standards or elective per management decisions.

Types of Financial Disclosures

Accounting Changes

If a corporation makes a significant change to their accounting rules, such as a change in inventory valuation, depreciation procedures, or application of GAAP, they must disclose it. These types of disclosures explain readers of the financial statements of a company's financial information why certain numbers may appear to have changed.

Accounting Errors

Accounting errors can happen for a variety of causes including transposition, mathematical computation, and erroneous application of GAAP or neglecting to revalue assets using fair market value. When an error is identified, it must be corrected. This generally entails updating earlier period financial statements. This information must be noted in the disclosure. Keep in mind that serious accounting mistakes might lead to financial audits and even bankruptcy for the organisation.

Asset Retirement

When the asset is no longer useful to the company, it is retired. The procedure for retiring an asset involves the organisation to secure both a fair market value and salvage value for the asset. An asset's net loss occurs when the sale price falls below the asset's salvage value. The net loss is then included on the company's income statement, which is then explained via a disclosure.

Insurance Contract Modifications

A company's balance sheet is affected by changes to insurance contracts. Because companies use the balance sheet to determine the total economic value added by their business. In order to explain why the insurance contract was changed and what current or future consequences may arise, a financial disclosure is necessary. A business owner's life insurance policy or general liability insurance are two examples of insurance contracts.

Other items

Other items requiring disclosure are noteworthy events and transactions. These events are infrequent but made a significant impact on the current financial period.

Methods of Making a Disclosure

Disclosures may be basic statements noting the change or provide a long explanation for the rationale to change the company's accounting rules and practises.

According to GAAP and SEC guidelines, voluntary disclosure in accounting is when a company's management provides information that is not required but is thought to be significant to annual report readers' decision-making that goes above and beyond what is required by law.

Investors, companies, and the economy all gain from voluntary disclosure; for example, it improves capital allocation decisions and lowers the cost of capital for businesses. Voluntary disclosure of financial information has been recommended by Chau and Gray (2002 and others) and others.

•

MODULE-2

IDENTIFYING CLIENT NEED AND OBJECTIVE

The step of acquiring data is critical since it is impossible to make well-informed decisions without correct data. The financial planner conducts a thorough evaluation of all pertinent data and papers at this stage.

The time you take compiling this information will allow us to cut to the point in putting together next steps to help you make your dreams a reality. The overview of your assets and responsibilities, your ambitions, and your dreams all connect with a strong financial strategy.

After establishing the client/planner relationship, the financial planner will set about determining the client's needs objectives and aspirations. These can be interlinked, but broadly:

A need is a requirement for capital and/or income that the client may have in the event of, say, death or illness to maintain their and/or their dependants' standard of living;

An objective is the amount of capital and/ or income that the client may require in the future to meet defined expenditure (e.g. providing income in retirement, paying for a child's wedding, purchasing a house or holiday home etc.);

An aspiration is something that the client would like to achieve in the future, but it is not as firm as an objective. Over time, aspirations may become objectives. An example of an aspiration could be "it would be nice to take a cruise when we retire".

Even where clients have clear goals in mind, they can sometimes have unrealistic expectations of what can be achieved or misconceptions about one area or another. During the fact-finding process the planner may also identify needs that the client was unaware of or had not considered, typically in the area of financial protection. Other needs commonly overlooked include the need to replace a company car on retirement or redundancy, or the additional costs involved in education planning, such as books, uniforms or school trips.

One way of differentiating between objectives and aspirations is to check whether they are SMART – Specific, Measurable, Achievable, Realistic, and Timescale. An objective must be SMART, whereas an aspiration is unlikely to be.

With most clients facing budget constraints to one degree or another and often unable to address all of their objectives initially, one or more objectives may need to be sacrificed, scaled back or postponed, although how many and to what extent won't become clear until after the planner has carried out their full analysis. The next section on prioritization deals with this in more detail.

PRITORIZING NEEDS AND OBJECTIVES

Most clients will have multiple needs and objectives but will usually not be in a position to address them all at the same time. As such they will need help in prioritizing which are the most important and which should be postponed or even sacrificed.

Most clients realize that they may not be able to afford to achieve all of their needs and objectives, so they may need to think about which may be the most important to achieve.

Whilst the prioritization should be the client's choice (to ensure that each objective remains the client's objective), the PIPSI acronym may help.

Protection
Income Protection
Pensions
Savings
Investment.

GATHERING PERSONAL INFORMATION

Typically, the fact-finding process starts with gathering personal information such as:

Name
Address
Phone number(s)
Email address
Date of birth
Marital status
Family and financial dependants
State of health
Smoker status
Residence/domicile for tax

A client's name and address need to be confirmed through documentary evidence to comply with Anti -Money Laundering regulations and typically a separate form of identity will be required to prove both name and address, for example a passport or driving licence as evidence of name and a recent utility bill or bank statement as evidence of address. Some firms are able to confirm identity via an electronic check, although this will normally be for individual, UK resident clients only.

Email addresses are particularly useful, as corresponding by email will allow a client to answer in their own time and attach documents that the planner may require for information or analysis. Email correspondence can also help to avoid misunderstandings in future as there will be a written record of the email conversation.

Once you move into the area of marital status, family and health it may be useful to explain to the client why this personal information is needed – some clients may have complex family.

GATHERING FINANCIAL INFORMATION

The financial planner will then require details of the client's:

Income
Employment or Self-Employment

Expenditure
Assets
Liabilities

The planner will need to determine the client's total income from all sources. As well as the gross figures, their net income after Income Tax and National Insurance contributions will need to be ascertained. This will help determine the surplus income available to commit to their financial planning needs once their expenditure is taken into account and can also be used as a check to ensure that the client is paying the right level of income tax.

It is also important to differentiate income from different sources, which will be relevant in a number of ways. As an example when planning for retirement, the planner will need to determine the level of 'UK relevant earnings' the client has, as the amount of tax relief they can have on their pension contributions is normally restricted to the higher of £3,600 or 100% of UK relevant earnings. The definition of relevant earnings however excludes rental income, investment income and dividend income, all of which might make up part of a client's total income position.

Clients in employment are likely to have a number of benefits and possibly benefits in kind in addition to their basic salary. Over the course of the next few years, as automatic enrolment is fully implemented, it will be less common to come across clients who are not members of an employer pension scheme. Employed clients may also benefit from a death-in-service benefit, which would typically pay out a multiple of salary on their death. Other common benefits they may be entitled to include Private Medical Insurance, Income Protection, as well as Save as You Earn schemes or Share Incentive Plans which may impact on tax planning. Clients may also receive regular bonuses or commissions which could, for example, be taken into account when applying for a mortgage.

These benefits will need to be taken into account when determining whether the client has any shortfalls in their retirement provision or financial protection needs for example, so it is vital to get accurate information on all of these benefits. In some cases, a client may even need to be advised to opt out of their employer pension scheme to avoid breaching the annual or lifetime allowance for pension.

The financial planner must be able to help clients identify their financial objectives and to develop them into clearly definable and measurable goals.

CLIENT EXPECTATION

Clients need to like working with their financial advisor. They need to feel comfortable sharing personal information. They expect their advisor to **be human and show empathy** (even sympathy) as the situation warrants. Integrity—this is the core, the essence, of the client-financial advisor relationship.

CLIENT OBJECTIVES

Objectives are minor steps that can be completed by a customer in order to attain the plan goal. Each time a client achieves a target, they feel that they are progressing. Activities may be paid for by the agency, for example a counselling service.

FOR EX- Success in a drug discovery project can only be achieved if there is a knowledge of client objectives, scheduling, and available resources to reach realistic and stated targets. Provide has the skills and expertise to plan initiatives that have a high likelihood of success for our clients.

An early-stage discovery project's analysis and solution design might comprise the following:

- A study of project history, biology & chemistry \s• Assessment of viability and the prospect for innovative intellectual property creation
- Evaluation of difficulties, opportunities, and competitive landscape With this backround, we next move to:

- Develop a project plan to be monitored and coordinated between Proved and the client
- Propose a research programme that is staged and comprises go/no go decision points. Establish the most efficient way to utilise the Alliance team and outside resources in order to meet the goals of the client
- Listen closely and let clients talk; you may find out something you never thought about asking. Inquire about the person's current interests and previous pastimes. Gently help your clients to take responsibility for their own problems/needs.

NEED OF FINANCIAL PLANNING

Many people have the same question running through their minds: do they need a financial strategy? Definitely. The financial plans of each individual must be made clear to them. If you're running a family or a business, financial planning can help you solve challenges more effectively.

In the event of a financial emergency, you will be better prepared to handle the situation. It's like a mini-roadmap that helps you navigate the procedure.

Financial planning is a process, not a product. Your money will be better managed over time, and you'll be better prepared for life's inevitable financial setbacks with this long-term strategy.

1. Income Management

One of the most important benefits of financial planning is that it may actually assist you in making the most effective use of your financial resources. It can also assist you in building a strategy that will assist you in calculating the quantity of resources needed for monthly spending.

Tax planning is made easier when you know exactly how much money you'll need and how much you'll be able to save.

Anyone can profit from this, whether they are a company or an individual.

2. Improved Cash Flow

Income growth leads to a rise in overall retained earnings. In both your work and personal life, it's critical to have a financial planning in place so that you can fulfil a range of obligations as they emerge. Analyzing your spending patterns and creating a budget will help you rapidly identify areas where you need to devote more time and energy.

This form of expenditure prioritising can substantially assist you in keeping track of your working capital, lowering overhead costs, and ultimately raising your overall capital.

3. for Better Investment

A well-thought-out financial strategy takes into account your unique circumstances, level of risk tolerance, and long-term objectives. It then aids you in selecting the ideal financial choices in light of your requirements and goals. Financial planning aids in the construction and planning of financial resources for the future.

It is possible to save money no matter what your age or profession is at Canara HSBC Oriental Bank of Commerce. You can choose from Savings Plans to Term Insurance plans that provide a heap of benefits to the buyer and family depending on the plan you have chosen.

4. Enhanced ROI on Portfolio

Financial decisions, risk assessments, cash management, liability management, and goal planning are key components of financial planning. Financial planning allows you to develop an integrated investment programme that takes into consideration your goals, appetite for risk, and available liquidity, allowing you to enhance the return on your portfolio.

5. Inflation Secured

Inflation has been named the "greatest killer of buying power." Over the preceding few decades, the value of money has declined drastically. In the foreseeable, it is only projected to deteriorate.

As a result, it is vital to plan your finances for a brighter and more secure future. With diligent financial preparation, you'll be better equipped to deal with increased inflation in the coming years as your firm becomes older.

6. Guarded Retirement Plan

While accomplishing your family's aims is a frequent ambition for a comfortable post-retirement existence. If you want to retire early, you should start investing as soon as possible because compounding works best when money is invested for a longer period of time.

When bills remain but income dries up, smart financial planning aids you in developing an appropriate corpus for retirement. To reach your long-term goals, it's generally a good idea to begin investing as early as possible.

A well-structured approach to financial planning also enables clients to explore their problems and facilitates the development of several solutions to help them achieve their goals. To be effective, the procedure must take into account all of a customer's concerns.

FINANCIAL SITUATION

Typical markers of great financial health include a regular flow of income, rare changes in expenses, strong returns on investments that have been made, and a cash balance that is rising and is on pace to continue to increase.

Basics of Financial Planning

Financial Planning is the process of accomplishing your life goals through the right management of your resources. Life objectives can include buying a house, preparing for your child's further education or planning for retirement.

Determine Your Current Financial Situation

Stage-In this first step of the financial planning process, you will determine your present financial condition with reference to income, savings, living expenses, and debts. Getting a handle on your current financial situation by compiling a list of all of your assets, liabilities, and expenditures is a good starting point for any future financial planning efforts.

Step 2: Develop Financial Goals

You should frequently review your financial values and aspirations. This involves identifying how you feel about money and why you feel that way. The objective of this analysis is to identify your necessities from your wants.

Financial planning requires a clear understanding of one's financial objectives. Regardless of what other people tell you about setting financial goals, it is ultimately up to you to select which of those goals you want to pursue. Your financial goals can range from spending all of your present money to building an intensive savings and investment programme for your future financial security.

Step 3: Identify Alternative Courses of Action

Developing alternatives is vital for making smart selections. Although numerous circumstances will influence the available possibilities, feasible courses of action usually fall into these categories:

- Continue the same course of action.
  This situation should be developed.
  It's time to get things back to normal.
- Take a fresh line of action.
- Not all of these categories will apply to every choice scenario; nevertheless, they do reflect alternative courses of action.
- Creativity in decision making is key to effective selections. Considering all of the various choices will help you make more productive and fulfilling judgments.

Step 4: Evaluate Alternatives

- In order to determine the best course of action, you must analyse your personal position, your ideals, and the state of the economy.
- Consequences of Choices. Every decision cuts off alternatives. For example, a decision to invest in stock may mean you cannot take a trip. A decision to go to school full time may mean you cannot work full time. is what you give up by making a choice. This cost, generally referred to as the trade-off of a decision, cannot always be measured in cash.
- What you give up when you make a decision is called the "opportunity cost." This cost, generally referred to as the trade-off of a decision, cannot always be measured in cash.
- Your financial and personal position will necessitate constant decision-making on your side. Thus, you will need to examine the missed possibilities that will come from your selections.

Evaluating Risk

- Every decision is accompanied by some degree of uncertainty. Selecting a college degree and choosing a job field involve risk. What if you don't enjoy or can't find work in this field?
- Other decisions involve a very minimal degree of risk, such as placing money in a savings account or purchasing products that cost only a few dollars. Your chances of losing something of considerable worth are low in these instances.
- In many financial decisions, detecting and analysing risk is challenging. The best method to consider risk is to obtain information based on your experience and the experiences of others and to use financial planning information sources.

Financial Planning Information Sources

- Relevant information is necessary at each level of the decision-making process.

Step 5: Create and Implement a Financial Action Plan

- Creating an action plan is the goal of this step in the financial planning process. This requires picking approaches to reach your aims. As you achieve your immediate or short-term goals, the goals next in importance will come into view.

To accomplish your financial action plan, you may need assistance from others. For example, you may use the services of an insurance agent to obtain property insurance or the services of an investment broker to purchase stocks, bonds, or mutual funds.

Step 6: Reevaluate and Revise Your Plan

Financial planning is a dynamic process that does not cease when you take a particular step. You need to frequently examine your financial decisions. Changing personal, social, and economic conditions may demand more regular assessments. When life events influence your financial demands, this financial planning approach will give a vehicle for reacting to those changes. This decision-making process can help you make priority adjustments to your financial objectives and activities in keeping with your current living situation if you evaluate it on a regular basis.

Your financial decisions will have more direction and purpose if you have done your planning. It gives you a better idea of the ripple effect your financial decisions will have on the rest of your life. Buying a particular investment product might help you pay off your mortgage sooner or it might add corpus to your retirement significantly. By Viewing each financial action as part of the whole, you can examine its short- & long-term effects on your life goals.

FINANCIAL PLANNING IN INDIA

India is one of the world's developing economies. Once it comes to investment funds, India seems to have a strong credit rating, but it was constrained to safeguarding cash flows in the presumed safe fields of gold, property development, bank accounts, and others.

But if you don't have a strategy in place before you invest, what's the point? Only when investments are created and maintained with sufficient financial planning do they meet one's life goals, giving one's equity investment guidance and focus. Financial planning is still very much in the early phases of development in India.

According to a Standard & Poor's worldwide financial literacy assessment, barely 24 percent of Indians are economically literate. It means that 76% of Indians aren't familiar with the basics of financial literacy. In addition, we've never wavered in our faith in gold and real estate.

Individual investors struggle to believe in financial planning as a theory since it demands a long-term commitment on their behalf. The state has certainly established the National Centre for Financial Education (NCFE) to increase financial literacy across diverse segments of the populace.

A financial planning ensures you are in complete command of your finances, income and duties while also providing you with a clear understanding of your options should something unexpected happen. In a nutshell, financial planning empowers you to take command of your life and destiny.

•

MODULE-3

FINANCIAL PLANNING

Financial planning is a way of creating an action plan to meet our current and future financial needs according to our financial situation. Financial planning is important. Even the best financial planners around the world use 6 strategies of financial planning.

FINANCIAL NEEDS OF INDIVIDUALS

Humans are the most civilized living beings on earth which requires good food, shelter and basic goods to survive, All of these require money.

You can realize these needs in different ways. Some needs are of short duration and some are needed after a long time. It is important to know all types of needs for better financial planning.

1. **Daily needs** – These are the requirements we need every day.
2. **Medical Needs** – Needs treatment after falling ill.
3. **Emergency Needs** -Needs which are associated with very bad times of life.
4. **Needs of Children Education** – The best education of children is one of your priorities.
5. **Needs have owned home** – I think everybody needs a beautiful house.
6. **Needs related to marriage of children**
7. Needs after retirement
8. Needs when the earning head of the family / survivor is not alive

9. Extra needs we feel– needs of different life style related things like T.V., Computer, A.C., Freeze, Car, Visiting overseas or elsewhere. Actually these are wants.

Of course, some of these needs vary from person to person. But there are definitely requirements.

A financial plan is a report of your current income, long-term and short-term goals, and the ways or potential investments to achieve those goals. The efficiency of any financial plan can be determined by the investment amount and time to hit your targets. To plan and implement a valuable financial strategy, it is crucial to analyze its components.

FIVE COMPONENTS OF A FINANCIAL PLAN

Financial planning is an important aspect of our lives. Buying the best savings plan to boost your financial planning is not the only solution. Here are five components of a financial plan:

1. Goal Identification

You must understand and identify your desires and goals. The efficiency of the plan depends on the clarity of your aims. Listing down your goals might assist you in getting clarity.

a. Short-term: Goals that you want to achieve in the next 5 years are considered short-term goals. Settlement of antecedent debts, purchasing luxury or small assets.
b. Medium-term: Become an entrepreneur, purchasing property and other goals with a high investment amount that you plan to fulfil in 5-10 years.
c. Long-term goals: The period of long-term goals is considered to be more than 10 years. Retirement, education are some of the basic long-term goals.

Goals often sometimes appear to be unachievable. It requires strong planning and clarity to minimize the gap between your goals.

2. Listing Assets and Liabilities

Listing down assets and liabilities gives a clear picture of your current financial value. Products or materials you possess and could bargain to raise capital are considered assets. The property, stocks, jewellery, vehicle, machinery, etc., you own are your assets.

Note that vehicles and machinery are examples of depreciating assets. Liabilities are the debts, mortgage property, and unpaid loans. The three different types of Liabilities are:

a. Current liabilities: Debts that are to be settled in a short period, i.e. one year in most cases.
b. Non-current liabilities: These are long-term liabilities that are to be paid over a few years.
c. Contingent liabilities: Occurring of liabilities depends on the outcomes of events that are to be held in the future. Also, there is an equal probability of the liability to arise depending on the circumstances.

3. Cash Flow and Expense Monitoring

An income statement or bank account statement gives a complete overview of your income as well as your expenses. Cash flow is the amount of money increasing and egressing your bank account. Salary, return on investment, etc., are some of the permanent forms of income. Temporary or unstructured income is bonuses, rewards, dividends on stocks.

Expense is the amount you are bound to spend; expense can be grouped as necessity and luxury. Setting up the ratio of needs, wants and savings might help you plan structure or cash flow. 5:3:2 is the widely accepted ratio.

Needs include monthly rent, EMI’s, grains and groceries, fuel or travel expenses, repairs, etc. Luxuries are resources that are not on the top of your priority list and are less essential are called luxury. Some of the best examples are dining out, cinema halls, subscription plans.

4. Insurance Planning

A fixed amount of your salary might be considered investment money or an emergency fund. Insurance policies could be the potential assets that would support you in unfortunate and tough times. Selecting the type of insurance policies depends on the goals you are planning to achieve. The most common and popular insurance plans are:

*a. **Term Life Insurance Plan***

Term life insurance plans are one of the simplest and affordable insurance plans that you can purchase. The policy covers death risk, and the maturity amount is transferred to the nominee in case of the applicant's death. The benefits of the term insurance can be stretched via purchasing add-ons.

*b. **ULIP***

Unit-linked insurance plans are abbreviated as ULIP. This policy comes with three levels of benefits: insurance coverage, wealth expansion, tax-saving. ULIPs are customizable according to your investment and insurance requirements.

*c. **Child Plan***

Being a parent, you might be under constant stress worrying about your child's future. Child insurance plans cover every stage of your child's life, from higher studies, foreign studies, weddings, etc.

*d. **Retirement Plan***

These insurance policies are your income source after your retirement. They are long-term policies and mature after the age of 65 in India. The payouts of retirement plans can be one time or in parts, i.e. monthly or quarterly. A retirement plan gives you the security to live independently.

Learn how to start planning for your retirement.

An important point to note that all insurance plans can be claimed by the nominee in case of any unfortunate death of the applicant. Also, the premium, rate of interest, additional benefits vary from bank to bank.

5. Monitoring and Optimization

It is the only way to confirm that your current plans are effective and growing in a positive direction. Keeping a regular check on your assets, enrolled plans, and invested stocks and mutual funds. Using your valuable assets to increase the liquidity ratio.

Analyzing your expense to income ratio and cutting down the overhead expenses for future investment. Goals are the final product of your investment, and there are times when you might experience that your goals can be more structured and optimized.

In such situations restructuring, your current plans would be a wise decision. One such example is to plan an early retirement; you can customize your premium amount and request for early maturity.

STRATEGIES OF FINANCIAL PLANNING

Strategy 1: Setting Financial Goals and Objectives

First of all, you take a pen and note all the goals that you want to achieve in your life. It is possible that some of them may not need a goal. But you also write it, since you want to get it.

After making the list, analyze your goals one by one. Which goal is currently important? Which goal will be the priority later? Decide the objectives of all the goals.

Recognize the difference between needs and desires from those goals. You should identify your current expenses. Then think about comprehensive savings for future security and set goals to invest the money saved.

Strategy 2: Evaluate Where You Stand Financially

This is a difficult task because you are facing yourself. After setting the goals you should first prepare a list of assets and liabilities you already have. Your liabilities column should be small and the column of assets should be large.

Assets tend to increase your income over time while liability reduces income.

Write the current values of all of them. Keep an eye on money inflows and outflows. For that use flow diagrams. All these steps enable you to evaluate your current financial situation correctly.

Strategy 3: Analyze the Data you've gathered

This is an important step where you have to thoroughly examine all the data collected. You require data analysis to check their feasibility. Pay attention on the priorities and values which seems not to be fulfilling in certain time frame.

Use financial calculator to ease your calculations. This will enable you to know how much amount to save and invest to achieve a certain goal.

For example, if you want your home after 20 years from today and if it costs 50 lakh, then a financial calculator will help you know how much money you should save and invest every month.

If you find your present income is not enough to achieve some goals. Then follow next step.

Strategy 4: Identify Alternative Sources of Income

Your regular income is a major source of meeting your needs. But in most cases it has been seen that they are not sufficient. In such circumstances it becomes important to look for some alternative source of income.

There are plenty of opportunities to make money by a side hustle which can be an active or passive source of income. Identify it according to your interest, ability and convenience.

Strategy 5: Develop and Implement Final Plan

After following the above four steps, you can easily develop the final plan. This is not a complicated mathematical calculation. This is a matter related to the future of you and your family.

Which you do with seriousness. You also get to know a lot about yourself.

Strategy 6: Periodically Review and Revise

There is a chance of uncertainty everywhere.

Everything does not happen according to us and you. Once you start implementing it after doing financial planning, you might not get 100% results. But you have progressed towards success.

Do not be disappointed. From time to time (almost once in a year), you keep reviewing these 6 strategies of financial planning. And if you feel necessary, modify it.

PRESENTING AN IMPACTFUL FINANCIAL PLAN

A financial plan provides a detailed picture of your current financial situation, your financial goals, and any tactics you've set in place to attain those goals. Detailed information on your finances, such as your cash flow, savings, debt, investments, and insurance, should be part of any sound financial strategy.

Your client's specific needs necessitate modifying the presentation. Here are five things you can adjust to meet the demands of your clients:

1. Summarize the client's objectives

This is the most important part of the process. Allows you to focus on the client's needs and make them feel like you're working with them.

At the beginning of the meeting, it will be easier to offer relevant solutions if the client's objectives are summarised.

2. Summarize the client's financial situation

In order to demonstrate to the client that you have a thorough comprehension of their financial condition, you should take this step. The summary may serve as a reminder for the client to provide you with additional information, and you can assess whether this additional information affects your analysis.

3. Explain the results of your analysis

Make sure your message is comprehended by tailoring it to your intended audience. Is the customer a driver, an artist, a thinker, or just a nice guy?

Drivers are eager to get to work as soon as possible. They value their time greatly. Make your financial plan clear and simple, focusing on the targets and the means that will be done to achieve them.

Clients who are open and honest are more likely to feel confident making decisions on their own. You don't have to follow the order of the document while presenting your financial prediction. Make sure they understand the strategy because they are intuitive and impulsive.

Data, dates, and reports are preferred by clients who are analytical in nature. Don't forget to describe all of your working hypotheses! Make sure to spend some time describing the plan's technique and, if necessary, providing the client with a few appendices and calculations sheets.

Clients that are easy to get along with have a sensitive nature and are wary of taking chances. They are, nevertheless, excellent listeners. Slowly and softly deliver your financial projections. They'll feel more at ease when it comes time to make a decision.

Simple graphs are the best method to show findings. Client assets and their changes over time should be shown in a graph.

Display the goal of the customer. Say, "Have money till I'm 96 years old and leave money to my estate."

In the end, provide the investor with the solutions and methods they need in order to reach their retirement goals (review retirement age, reduce cost of living, increase savings, etc.).

4. Present strategies, recommendations and proposed solutions

It is crucial to examine your client's objectives in step 1 before making recommendations and proposing realistic solutions that will help them reach their goals.Due to the fact that most recommendations require a customer to alter their behaviour,

Personalize the recommendations if possible. A better way of putting it is to explain that RESPs can be utilised to help pay for a child's education instead of suggesting that they are the best way to do so.

5. Provide an action plan and an implementation schedule

Aim for immediate implementation of any recommendations you provide. Establish a follow-up date and action plan for any items that can't be implemented that day.

You also need to divide up the work among any outside experts you have hired (e.g., wills and estate lawyer, pension expert, tax specialist, etc.).

Your financial prediction is complete, and you're ready to go. Ensure that you communicate clearly and tactfully with your clients at all times. I wish you the best of luck with your presentation.

A financial plan serves as a map to help you navigate your way through life's twists and turns. When it comes to managing your finances, it is all about being in charge of your finances so that you may reach your goals. To achieve your objectives and aspirations, you must have enough money in your bank account.

CLIENT RISK TOLERANCE

As a result, a client's willingness to take on more risk is called his or her "risk tolerance." Capacity for Danger: The amount of risk a client can take without jeopardizing their goals The amount of risk that must be taken in order to satisfy a client's goals.

Risk tolerance is a combination of two factors. One is the **emotional willingness to face a loss** and the other financial capacity to absorb a loss without a change in lifestyle.

Client risk is the money laundering and terrorist financing (MLTF) and other financial crime risks potentially posed by a client – to which your firm may be exposed to. It is vital that the firm understands the risk posed by its clients. By doing this, an appropriate risk-based process can be implemented.

The amount of loss an investor may tolerate when making an investing decision is referred to as risk tolerance. A person's tolerance for risk is usually categorised into one of three broad groups: conservative, moderate, or aggressive. They are categorised as aggressive, moderate, or conservative.

The level of risk a client is ready to bear is known as their risk profile. When it comes to measuring a customer's risk profile, engaging the client in a cost-benefit analysis is not as straightforward as it sounds. The client has to decide how much he's willing to spend for security.

In financial planning, risk tolerance is the degree of volatility in investment returns that an investor is able to bear. Investing requires a certain level of risk tolerance. In general, those with a larger net worth and more disposable money can take more risks with their assets.

TIPS FOR ASSESSING A CLIENT'S RISK TOLERANCE

1. Talking to Clients. Close the Conversation Gap With Your Clients.
2. Working with Client's Money. 4 Basic Pointers When Investing Other People's Money.
3. Talking about Difficult Topics. Talk About Financial Constraints to Your Clients.
4. The Investing Landscape. ETFs vs.

FACTORS THAT INFLUENCE RISK TOLERANCE

1. Timeline

A distinct time horizon will be used by each investor based on their plans. Aspects of Investing Investors use the term "investment horizon" to describe the length of time they plan on holding on to their investments before selling them for a profit. Many factors influence an individual's ability to invest in the long term. However, the most important consideration is the amount of risk the investor is willing to take. If you have more time, you can generally take greater risks. At fifteen years from now, someone who needs a given sum of money can take more risk than someone who needs that sum of money in five years. It's because the market has been rising steadily throughout the years. However, the short-term lows are persistent.

2. Goals

Personal financial goals varies from one person to the next. Having the most money isn't the only goal of financial planning for many people. An investing strategy is devised based on the amount of money needed to achieve a specific goal. Return on Investment In financial terms, the Rate of Return (ROR) is the percentage change in an investment's value over time compared to its starting cost. In this guide, you'll learn about the most common formulas that are used. Based on their personal goals, each person will have a varied risk tolerance.

3. Age

Young people are usually more willing to take risks than their elders. Young people have the opportunity to earn more money and have more time to deal with market swings since they are more flexible.

4. Portfolio size

The more risk tolerant you are, the more money you have in the bank. Having a $50 million portfolio will allow an investor to take greater risks than an investor with a $5 million portfolio. A larger portfolio's loss is less than a smaller portfolio's loss because of the larger size of the portfolio.

5. Investor comfort level

Risk is handled differently by each investor. It's reasonable for some investors to be more willing to take risks than others. On the other hand, for some investors, market volatility can be exceedingly upsetting. A person's willingness to take risks, in turn, depends on their risk tolerance.

Types of Risk Tolerance

A person's tolerance for risk is usually categorised into one of three broad groups: conservative, moderate, or aggressive. Only a few of the elements that go into assigning each category have been mentioned as follows:

1. Aggressive

Investors that take on aggressive risk are well-versed in the market and aren't afraid to take big chances. Investors like this are accustomed to experiencing significant fluctuations in their portfolios. Investors who are aggressive tend to be well-off, well-versed, and well-diversified.

They choose equities and other asset classes that have a high degree of volatility. Securities that are traded on the open market. Marketable securities, or investments that may be traded on the open market, are known as public securities. Either equity or debt is used to value the securities. It's not uncommon for them to see big gains when the market is doing well and massive losses when it isn't doing so well. In the event of a market crisis, however, they do not panic-sell because they are used to market volatility on a regular basis.

2. Moderate

Investors that take a moderate risk take less risk than those who take a more aggressive risk. A percentage of losses is frequently set as a limit for the amount of risk they are willing to take. They invest in a variety of hazardous and secure asset classes. The Asset Type The term "asset class" refers to a group of investment instruments that share many characteristics. They are normally traded in the same financial markets and are subject to the same rules and regulations as other securities. When the market goes up, they make less money than aggressive investors, but they don't suffer massive losses when it goes down.

3. Conservative

The most risk-averse investors are known as "conservatives." They avoid dangerous investments at all costs and stick to solutions that they believe are the most secure. Avoiding losses is more important to them than gaining money. They only invest in a few asset classes, such as FDs and PPFs, which protect their capital.

Risk assessment explained

the financial planning risk assessment is measured under three headings:

1. Attitude to risk

This assesses the client's grasp of risk and how it applies to their personal and financial lives.

2. Tolerance for risk

This is an attempt to determine how much volatility a client is willing to accept and witness throughout the course of an investment.

3. Capacity for risk

In the event of a huge gain or loss in an investment, this quantifies the clients' ability to tolerate the loss or their rate of change in financial circumstances.

THE FORMAL PROCESS TO ASSESS A FINANCIAL CLIENT'S RISK PROFILE

Your insurance plan should include these five phases, regardless of the method you employ to arrive at a dollar figure for insurance purposes:

Step 1: Assess the client's exposure to risk

Risk assessment is an activity in determining the worst-case scenario for a client's exposure to risk. In order to answer this question, you and your customer must address the following areas:

What would happen if the primary breadwinner died? Do you know how much a funeral would cost?

Health and illness: Is there a family history of some deadly diseases? Are certain members of the family more susceptible to bodily harm or sickness than others? In the event of a long-term illness in the family, what would happen to the family's finances?

• Loss of a job: How would a job loss affect the family's financial situation? Is your customer financially prepared in the event of a layoff?

In the event that a breadwinner is unable to work, how would this affect the family's finances?

Divorce: What is the financial impact of divorce? • Marriage: What is the financial impact of marriage?

With regard to your client's family members, what financial dangers do they pose? For example, treatment and intervention for substance misuse can be expensive.

Is there anything that could be taken from the family home in the event of a natural disaster? A vehicle could be totaled, what would you do? Items of value could be taken, what if?

It is important to consider the financial implications of a family business in the event it is damaged or destroyed. Suppose a consumer brought a lawsuit against the company for damages.

Some or all of these losses may already be covered by your client's existing plans or policies. Now that you have a better understanding of his ability to deal with potential losses, you may help him become more conscious of what he could lose should certain sad situations occur.

Step 2: Educate the client on mitigating risks

the appropriateness of allocating some of the client's assets to guard against prospective losses, even if you can't place a price tag on risk. Here is the formula I follow:

Financial loss Present Value (PV) = PV – PV – PV - PV of all premiums + Opportunity Cost (if applicable)

Where,

Present value of future, potential, and/or likely liabilities in dollars is called PV economic loss.

The PV sum of all premiums paid is the total sum of all premiums paid throughout time to protect against that specific future liability.

• The money that could have been made if the insurance premiums were invested somewhere else is known as the "opportunity cost." (Assume a 5% to 6% compounded return.)

Amounts that can be accessed at some point in the future, assuming that feature is applicable, are known as the PV of cash value accumulations (CPV).

If a loss were to occur, your client's overall insurance costs would exceed the total cost of the damage. If you'd like to go even farther, you may conduct a statistical analysis of the likelihood that your client would die or become disabled. But there's a snag: no one believes it might happen to him, therefore doing the probability exercise with clients is a waste of time.

Step 3: Decide how much loss the client wants to protect against

Trade-offs are common when it comes to insurance because it isn't free. HealthCare.gov, for example, has a basic to platinum tier of coverage. When it comes to health insurance, if you're a healthy 25-year-old man, you're more likely to go for the bronze plan. A gold or platinum plan may be a better option for someone who is older and has a number of health conditions.

Step 4: Research insurance products

As soon as you and your client have agreed on what the potential loss is worth, you may begin shopping for insurance solutions to match your client's demands. Use the following criteria when making product recommendations while you're out shopping:

It is possible to narrow down your possibilities by working only with insurance providers that are financially strong. A company's financial health is a sign that its leadership is solid, its goods are top-notch, and it plans to expand and adapt in the future. Get a sense of a company's financial health by looking at their Comdex score. On most insurance providers' websites, you'll find this information. VitalSigns or EbixLife subscriptions are available to licenced insurance brokers, therefore you'll be able to access this data.

When comparing plans, look at the cost, coverage, and features of each to see which ones offer the most for your money. Additional perks, such as waivers of premiums if a client is very ill or incapacitated, are features. Don't neglect the importance of insurance policy features.

Choosing a life insurance policy can be a complicated process, therefore it's important to know if the policy or contract can be converted to a different type of insurance; for example, a term policy can be converted to a permanent policy later.

Present your client with options by finding at least one low-cost, midrange, and high-cost policy to choose from. If you decide to give a recommendation, do so only after performing your own product study in the competitive marketplace. There is nothing wrong with having a preference for a particular insurance company, but conduct a thorough competitive study and recommend policies that are actually in the best interest of your clients.

The final step is to present the possibilities, agree on a solution, and implement it.

Step 5: Present the options, reach agreement, and implement the plan

As illustrated, create a table to show your strategy for managing liability. For each solution you offer, explain why you think it's a viable alternative and present its benefits and drawbacks. Inform your customers that you have only worked with the top insurance firms, and emphasize the significance of only working with organisations that can afford to back their products.

Type	Pro	Con	Cost	Benefit	Features
Life Insurance	Protects household lifestyle	Poor health rating makes it expensive	$5,000/year level premiums for 20 years	$1,500,000 death benefit	Convertible into permanent policy after one year
Disability Income insurance	Accident prone breadwinner	Certain activities are excluded from coverage	$2,000/year level premiums, paid until age 65	$10,000/month until age 65, plus annual 2% inflation rider	Dividend participating policy, own occupation protected
Annuity	Pays a guaranteed income for life	Given a long life, income loses purchasing power	Total contract expenses are 2.75% of contract value per year	Guaranteed income of 5% starting at age 65, based on a guaranteed roll-up credited interest rate of 7% per year	Can be liquidated for cash value, up to 10% of contract value without back-end sales charge

ASSESSMENT OF OPTIONS IN FINANCIAL PLANNING

The purpose of a financial evaluation is to assist you determine if you are on track to achieve your financial goals. Assessing your financial condition and making plans for the future can be accomplished through the use of a financial evaluation.

A good financial goals assessment will most likely ask questions regarding:

- What you're now making and how much money you're spending.

- Basic financial health, including your current retirement and emergency savings, credit scores, loans, residual income, current liquid assets, and debts.
- Tax returns, past income, self employment documents (if applicable), bank account statements, and other assets.
- Additionally, there may be ongoing bills and other financial obligations, such as taking care of children or elderly family members.
- • Short and long-term goals, such as saving for college education, buying a car, downsizing a family home, or saving for a preferred retirement community, care home, or other residential care.
- Your current credit card payments, credit score, credit history, interest rates, debts, and credit situation.
- Other housing related expenses, like property tax payments and mortgages.

An in-depth or more personal financial assessment will have these considerations taken into account:

- Retirement choices that are accessible to you at work.
- It's important to consider your existing financial condition before making a decision on a new bank account.
- How you handle money and what you wish to improve on.
- For is, how much money you want to put away for the future and how much you want to spend on luxuries.
- What your Social Security payments will look like.

With a financial assessment, you'll be able to plan for the future more effectively. To get your retirement planning on track, take our financial evaluation below.

List Your Financial Goals

Creating a chart of your financial goals, making a financial assessment, and assigning a timeline to reach them will influence your investment strategy. Follow these steps to set your financial goals on your own or with an expert financial planner.

Financial Goals Assessment

When it comes to your retirement, what are the most essential personal goals that you have?

Your key retirement goals should be listed below with a time range and the associated costs.

Setting a deadline

Time horizon of 0 to 3 years.

• Three to ten years is a medium-term timeframe.

Long-term: 10 years and more

Calculate the total cost of each objective.

Short-term goals can be met by using today's costs and a retirement calculator for long-term goals.

Aim No. 2: Set a Timetable

When looking at a project, it's important to consider the following time frames:

A retirement calculator can be used for medium- and long-term goals, as well as short-term ones.

3rd Objective: Set a Deadline

When looking at a project, it's important to consider the following time frames:

Analyze the expense of each objective.

For short-term goals, use today's costs; for medium- and long-term goals, use a retirement calculator

Is it appropriate to save a certain amount of your family's income today? Why?

3. What do you believe is an appropriate interest rate for an

investment?
In what year do you plan to stop working?
Is there anything you want to do when you're older?
Are you concerned about saving for your future?
Are you aware of all of your government pension benefits?? Do you know how much money you'll get from Social Security?

If you were unable to work due to a disability, would you be able to maintain your current lifestyle with the money you have saved? After that?

8. How long do you intend to live? Why not ask about your partner's life expectancy as well?
As you set retirement goals, you can use the information you gather from our financial assessment questionnaire.

Retirement and Financial Goals to Consider

While approaching retirement, your financial assessment may appear a little drab. You'll have a different financial evaluation when you're nearing retirement. People in their 50s and older often have the following aims in mind: ifferent. People in their 50s and older have a number of common aspirations.

Maintain or improve lifestyle

For most people, retirement is a time for relaxation after a lifetime of hard labour. Maintaining or growing your investment portfolio and increasing your income are both necessary in order to keep up with inflation.

Prevent running out of money

For many, this is a key priority. People in their fifties and sixties are particularly concerned about having to continue to work, rely on their children for financial assistance, or return to the workforce. Investments that are more volatile than low-volatility investments like Treasury bonds might assist ensure that you have ample cash flow in your retirement years.

Increase wealth

Most of the time, this group's primary focus is on long-term asset growth, whether for their own benefit or the benefit of a loved one's descendants or a charitable organisation. A growth-oriented investment strategy is prevalent if you fall into this category.

Other times you may come across a financial assessment

With reverse mortgages, every borrower must have a financial assessment done to verify that they can afford to pay property taxes and homeowners insurance over the life of the loan, according to federal regulations.

Lenders look at the borrower's sources of income, such as Social Security and pensions. Borrowers must submit certain papers, including tax returns and bank account statements.

A credit score issue will have to be explained. The lender must assess whether the explanation qualifies as an "extenuating circumstance" in getting the loan accepted.

Lenders examine financial assessments to see whether they must set aside a certain amount of money to pay for property taxes and other expenditures over the life of the loan, including residual income and the borrower's income. The "set aside" reduces the amount of loan money available to the borrower.

•

MODULE-4

IMPLEMENTATION OF FINANCIAL PLAN

Implementation duties agreed upon between the client and the financial planning expert are compatible with their scope of work and their ability to implement their suggestions, as well as their client's acceptance. Product and service suggestions are consistent with financial planning recommendations approved by the client when the financial planning expert is able to identify and present acceptable products and services.

Clients who have already completed our initial comprehensive financial planning process often return to us for assistance with implementing the modifications to their financial plan that we've recommended. We can help you in a number of ways.

Now that your financial strategy has been devised, it must be reviewed and, if necessary, revised before it can be put into effect. At this stage, we'll find and propose products and services that are in line with the financial planning advice that you've already agreed to.

Based on your goals and priorities, we will recommend the products and services that best suit your needs.

Time will always study qualitative and quantitative data and evaluate multiple tactics and goods that could fulfil your needs. Time will always review this information. As part of our financial planning recommendations, we may also make product or service recommendations. Typically, two visits are required to complete this process, which can either be done in person or over the phone.

Now, we'll start addressing the difficulties with insurance and estate planning that you've identified in your strategy. Referrals and coordination are available when legal, accounting, or actuarial experts are needed.

Moving forward fast and efficiently is our goal at this point; we'll handle the details while keeping you updated on the process.

Each step of the way will be customised to fit your time frame, tax rate, liquidity need, and risk tolerance. We're well aware that providing financial assistance is an on-going effort. As soon as it's created, we'll work with you to make sure you're on track to meet your goals.

The most difficult part of implementing a plan is that it's still a paper document, even if it's a well-thought-out one. For a business, this is one of the most difficult processes in financial planning because of the complexities involved. Putting the plans into action and sticking to them calls for a great deal of concentration and self-control. To carry out the mission as intended, everyone's cooperation is required.

The financial planner must also persuade everyone involved to stick with the strategy.

5 steps to financial planning success

Step 1 - Defining and agreeing your financial objectives and goals

The financial plan will be guided by your goals and objectives, which should serve as a blueprint for your financial future. The following should be included:

- measurable and attainable
- Definable and time-bound
- Make a distinction between your necessities and your desires.

To help you keep track of your progress, you should have them agreed upon and documented with your financial advisor.

They should also be examined on a regular basis to ensure that they are still relevant in light of current events.

Step 2 – Gathering your financial and personal information
How well your financial advisor is able to help you is directly related to how well you express your goals and financial situation to them.

Your financial advisor will conduct a thorough fact-finding session to gather all pertinent facts about your circumstances. • Income and expenditure • Assets and liabilities • Risk attitude, tolerance, and capacity will all be included in this section.

Step 3 – Analyzing your financial and personal information

Using the information you gave in step 2, your financial advisor creates a report that accurately reflects your current financial situation.

To help you better understand your financial situation and identify areas of strength or weakness, the following ratios have been compiled:

Ratios of Solvency, Savings, Liquidity, and Debt Service

Using a psychometrically constructed risk tolerance questionnaire, your attitude, tolerance, and capacity for risk are evaluated in respect to investment assets. Asset allocation for investment or pension goals can also be evaluated using this data set.

Step 4 – Development and presentation of the financial plan

It is through this data and analysis that the financial strategy is developed.

A recommendation should be made for each of the aims and objectives listed in step 1. Included in this report are the following items: (a balance sheet).

For the year-to-date consolidation of taxes

A cash flow statement for the year (displaying surplus or deficit)

Afterward, the report is signed by both the customer and their advisor.

Step 5 – Implementation and review of the financial plan

The adviser will present the suggested course of action once the analysis and creation of the strategy is complete. Changing loan providers or implementing a new pension or investment strategy may be necessary.

- Supplemental life or critical sickness insurance coverage.
- Changes in income and expenditures

The Adviser may carry out the recommendations or serve as your coach, coordinating the process with you and other specialists, such as accountants or investment managers, in order to help you achieve your goals. Financial product providers may also be handled by them.

It's important to keep an eye on your finances constantly, as they are constantly changing. The plan's goals should be revisited periodically to take into account changes in income, asset values, company or family situations, as well as other factors.

Conclusion

Following a clearly defined and documented strategy for financial planning will increase your chances for an effective conclusion significantly. In order to achieve both financial security and wealth, the correct analysis, dedication, and knowledge are required.

Coordination with Other Professionals

Clients and their advisors (estate planning attorneys, accountants, insurance consultants and bankers) work together to ensure that decisions are made in a timely manner. We'll work together with your other financial professionals to make sure everything's taken care of. It is our goal to provide you with referrals to specialists who are the best fit for your specific situation. As a rule, we don't take money for referring people to our site.

INVESTMENT ADVISOR

Is engaged in the business of compensation;

An investment advisor is someone who provides financial advice to clients. 202(a) (11) of the Act defines an investment adviser as anybody or firm that: provides advice to others or issues reports and analysis on securities;

Any individual, sole proprietor, partnership firm, company or body corporate can apply to be a Registered Investment Advisor (RIA) in India. Also, if the number of clients exceeds 150 members, then it is mandatory for an advisor to register with SEBI.

To qualify as a "fiduciary," an investment manager must be registered as an investment adviser, a bank or insurance business, and have acknowledged in writing that it is a fiduciary with respect to the plan in writing.

Banks, mutual fund companies, and insurance companies employ the majority of financial counsellors. They provide financial advice to both individuals and organisations in order to assist them in achieving their financial objectives.

A financial advisor is a person who gives advice on the best ways to invest your money. Whether it's an all-encompassing financial strategy or a series of smaller investments, the guidance they give can help you achieve your financial goals.

When it comes to making financial decisions, financial advisors can help with everything from selecting an investment vehicle to determining how often to conduct periodic reviews and, if necessary, enacting corrective steps.

Investment advisors generally monitor the performance of your investment, providing guidance about buying, selling, or holding investments. An investment advisor can either be a firm or an individual, but no matter what, the objective is to manage your investments and ensure they align with your overall investment strategy.

Investing advisors may provide some financial planning advice, but their primary role is to tell you which assets are most suited to your investment objectives.

You can engage an investing advisor who specialises in one area, such as trading options on a single stock, or you can get broad guidance and a portfolio built for you.

When it comes to fees for financial advisor services, they can range from a fixed fee to an hourly rate to a percentage of your investment gains.

When it comes to portfolio construction, wealth management-focused investment advisors address a number of distinct challenges. In particular, they could advise you on the following topics: what to invest in; whether to buy stocks or mutual funds; whether to invest in index funds or actively managed funds; which investments to use in retirement accounts; which investments to own in non-retirement accounts; what risks each investment entails; the expected return on your portfolio; and what types of taxable income you can expect from your investments. In order to lower your tax bill, you should think about how you can reorganise your investments.

NEED A FINANCIAL ADVISOR

Investing information is readily available on the internet, so why would you need a financial advisor?

It is because a financial advisor is a specialist in offering financial advice to customers based on his knowledge and their needs. While you may know what you need and how to get it, you may not always have the time to accomplish it all yourself. Here, a financial counsellor assumes all of the responsibility for your financial well-being.

Here are some benefits of engaging a financial advisor for your investment and financial planning needs:

Understanding your investment needs and chalking out a financial plan:

To begin the process of creating a financial plan, it is important to know the goal and necessity. You and your financial advisor work together to create a long-term financial strategy based on your requirements and goals.

Financial expertise:

A financial advisor brings knowledge of the financial markets to the table. A financial adviser or an investment advisor has to pass a series of exams and certifications before they can be called such. It's possible that working with a financial advisor to construct a portfolio, set goals, and track progress is a good idea.

Laying down SMART goals:

A goal needs to be SMART - measurable, achievable, realistic and time-bound – in order to succeed. Even in your financial plan, you need to set realistic goals based on your income, return expectations, and aspirations. This is something that a financial expert can assist you with.

Helping you choose the ideal path to being financially fit:

Your financial advisor can assist you in determining which investments are most suited to meet your goals. Depending on your risk-return objectives, your advisor will guide you in selecting the best financial product.

.

Regularly monitoring your portfolio:

A financial advisor helps you keep track of your investments because you may not have the time to do it on your own. To ensure that your investments are aligned with your financial goals, regular portfolio monitoring is essential.

Revising portfolio from time to time:

It is important to keep an eye on the market and changing needs when it comes to an investing portfolio. When this occurs, a consultant's knowledge and current market conditions would lead him to advise adjustments.

Fitness coaches and financial advisors have a lot in common: they both have a lot of experience, they both provide a solid fitness plan, and they both assist in monitoring and maintaining the long-term success of the plan.

How to Choose the Best Financial Advisor in India

SEBI Registered Investment Advisor (RIA)

SEBI is the regulatory authority for financial markets and services in India. SEBI mandates every individual/entity providing financial planning services to be registered with them. You may look up on **SEBI's website** for a complete list of SEBI RIAs. **Click here** to refer to Do's and Don't listed by SEBI as part of investor awareness. Always ensure that the entity you deal with is registered with SEBI.

Certified Financial Planner (CFP)

Certified Financial Planner (CFP) – The Financial Planning Standard Board (USA) has been certifying individuals who pass their stringent norms related to personal finance. This certification has worldwide recognition and is considered as the gold standard when it comes to helping individuals manage their finances. You can search for the Best Certified Financial Planners In India on **FPSB directory**.

Three Types of Financial Advisor

Flat Fee Only Financial Advisor

A Fee Only Financial Planner is someone who gets directly compensated by the investor. They charge for the financial plan and advisory services provided to the investor. They do not earn any commissions or brokerage from the products or strategies they recommend. There is no conflict of interest when the planner lists out the action items in a financial plan. They earn no kick backs or under the table payments for anything. These planners are bound by fiduciary responsibility and are mandated by SEBI to keep the best interests of the investors in mind.

Fee Based Financial Advisor

A Fee Based Financial Planner is someone who charges the investor for planning and might also receives commission from products or strategies recommended in the financial plan.

There are twin charges one for planning and one from investments. This is caused of concern as there is scope for potential conflict of interest from the products recommended in the financial plan.

Distributors of Financial Instruments

Distributors are involved in selling various investment instruments. They could be mutual funds, stocks, insurance products or any other financial instrument. Their income is generated from the commission or brokerage that is generated by selling those investments.

They are not mandated to ensure fiduciary responsibility and can naturally lead to huge conflicts of interest. Most people fall for their FREE services thinking that they are not paying anything, but fail to realize that the products recommended by them include costs in the form of high commissions. For example, such distributor recommends regular option of mutual funds instead of direct option where there are no commissions involved

STOCK BROKERS AND INSURANCE AGENTS

A stock broker's job is to make it easier for investors to buy and sell equities on the stock exchanges. The Indian stock markets can be traded through a number of well-known brokerages.

This third-party intermediary acts as a liaison between the seller of a particular security and its buyer. Big Stock is the source of this image. Because of this, when someone wants to acquire a bond or stock, their financial broker acts as the intermediary.

Traders in securities and commodities are known as stockbrokers, and they generally work directly with their clients. A stockbroker analyses a client's financial situation and then presents him with viable investment options. There are two ways for stockbrokers to trade stocks: either on the floor of the exchange market, or electronically.

To make money, a stockbroker constantly watches the financial market to see how different assets are performing, and then uses this information to make trades. A stockbroker's actions are likely to be influenced by corporate events such as mergers, public offers, annual financial statements, and acquisitions.

On the other hand, stockbrokers are constantly on the phone, trying to connect with existing and potential clients. People with strong customer service abilities will do well in this position. Additionally, stockbrokers must have excellent attention to detail and the ability to make swift decisions.

A stockbroker primarily deals in stock and commodity securities. Other self-financed products including insurance, bonds, and annuities can also be offered by financial counsellors.

Certified financial planners are held to a higher standard of ethics than non-certified financial planners, which requires them to put the interests of their clients first. Brokers, on the other hand, have no such requirement.

Financial products can and are sold by brokers and insurance agents (A, B and C mutual funds, annuities, variable life insurance, annuities). Their fiduciary care standard is based on "suitability." As long as their items are widely perceived to be "appropriate," they are OK to sell because they have a lower standard of care and may therefore earn more from product sales than the client.

Types of Stockbrokers

1. Full-Service Stockbroker

Customers of a full-service stockbroker have access to a wide range of financial products and services. Individual licenced stockbrokers are often allocated to each client. The research departments of the brokerage houses give analysts' recommendations and access to IPOs (IPOs) The first time a company goes public (IPO) It is the first time a corporation sells stock to the general public in an Initial Public Offering (IPO). Private companies are regarded to be non-public before an initial public offering (IPO), with a limited number of investors (founders, friends, family, and business investors such as venture capitalists or angel investors). Find out what an IPO stands for and how it works.

Full-service stockbrokers also include financial planning, business and personal home loans, banking services, and asset management. Clients have the option of contacting a personal stockbroker or using mobile and internet platforms to trade options.

Brokers who provide internet access and trading capabilities, on the other hand, demand greater commissions. There are fewer indications and tools for day traders on full-service stockbrokers' online platforms because long-term investors typically use them.

2. Discount Stockbroker

Discount stockbrokers offer a range of financial services, including the provision of quick and easy access to capital. Mutual funds are a type of investment vehicle. Investors pool their money into a mutual fund to invest in stocks, bonds, and other securities. Mutual funds are collectively owned and managed by a group of investors. The many types of funds, how they work, and the advantages and disadvantages of investing in them, banking products and other services are all covered in this section of the course. Compared to a full-service stockbroker, a cheap stockbroker offers a wide range of products and services for lower fees.

As a result, active swing and day traders may prefer

inexpensive stockbrokers. There are more research tools and trading options on the platforms for active day traders and investors than on full-service platforms.

3. Online Stockbroker

If you're an aggressive day trader, you'll benefit from an online stockbroker's low fees, which are typically charged per stock.

There are direct access systems that can route and chart trades, as well as access to numerous exchanges, market makers, and electronic communication networks, offered by online stockbrokerage firms (ECN).

Online stockbrokers also provide the advantages of accessibility and speed, allowing orders to be executed with a simple point-and-click method of operation. Options and stock orders can also be placed on the platforms. According to the volume of shares exchanged each month, software fees can be decreased or waived; however, the exchange fees must be paid in order to have access to heavy-duty platforms.

Qualifications of a Stockbroker

Education

If a stockbroker wants to work with an institutional client, an undergraduate degree in finance or business administration is essential. In addition, knowledge of accounting and forecasting procedures is required. Forecasting in the Finances Financial forecasting is the practise of anticipating how a company will perform in the future. Financial forecasting and planning, as well as relevant rules and regulations, are covered in this document.

Experience

There are many ways to become a stockbroker, including as an intern at a brokerage firm. However, in order to become a stockbroker, one needs have a thorough knowledge of accounting standards and financial market rules.

Exams

Financial Industry Regulatory Authority (FINRA) requires stockbrokers to pass the General Securities Representative Exam (FINRA). To be financed, a person must work with a FINRA member firm or a Self-Regulatory Organization (SRO) .

INSURANCE AGENTS

Only "appropriate" financial goods are required from financial advisors because they represent themselves or their organisation, not their clients' specific circumstances.

An insurance agent who's also a financial advisor can provide a holistic approach to financial planning. It's like consolidating your financial team from two people into one: Rather than having a financial planner and an insurance agent, you have one person who can do both jobs.

Renewing commissions are one of the major advantages of working as an insurance salesman. As the agent gains more and more clients, the cost of these renewals grows. For a long period of time, they can be extremely lucrative for the representative, almost like an annuity!

Because they know that the insurance representative is protecting them in the event of a disaster while the broker's job is to help their client make more money, there are more chances for brokers to lose their clients' money than for an insurance representative to keep their clients from losing their money.

Insurance agents may not receive their commissions if the client does not meet or is unwilling to satisfy certain health standards, but a broker receives a commission the moment a client pays for a stock.

Health, whole life, term life, and variable life insurance are only some of the products that most insurance firms offer; however, advisors have the ability to sell shares or debt instruments from literally thousands of publicly traded corporations.

Individuals who have young families at home are especially susceptible to burnout because insurance reps like to make appointments in the evenings when people are home from work.

•

MODULE-5

MONITORING THE FINANCIAL PLAN

When it comes to financial monitoring in projects, having regular and accurate financial reports is essential. This course is designed to help you learn more about how to monitor financial records and information effectively.

Clients who monitor their financial plans are more likely to be financially secure in the future. When a financial plan is kept current with a client's present condition, the client's involvement in his or her own financial well-being rises.

An vital part of financial management is a regular examination of activities to discover errors, anomalies, potential compliance issues, and large budget variations. By ensuring that transactions are precise and appropriate, the university's risk is minimised.

Checks on unit objectives, external constraints, and university designations are critical to ensure that funds are spent in accordance with expectations and that the amounts posted are reasonable.

As a financial manager, you should perform regular (at least monthly) financial review of your organization. Then research, validate, and when necessary, correct any issues that may arise. Sometimes issues may require further analysis, at which point you should contact the relevant departments and University offices, including the Office of the Provost and the Office of Finance and Treasury.

As a result, you will have more confidence in making both short-term and long-term financial decisions. As a result, the company benefits and expands at a faster rate. Their capacity to use the data they collect to move the business ahead is a critical component of their success.

REVIEW THE PROFRESS OF PLAN WITH CLIENT

Program administrators, planners and implementers; policymakers; and donors all rely on it to make educated judgments about the functioning of their programmes. In order to get the most out of your resources, you need to keep an eye on them and evaluate them.

Progress evaluations are a terrific way to recognise your clients' achievements if you keep an eye on and encourage them. As a result of reviews, you'll be able to identify the elements that helped or hampered your clients' goals, and you'll endeavour to lessen or remove those factors that hindered their success.

An opportunity to dig in and figure out what is working and what isn't with a customer can be found in progress reviews. By far, this is one of the most effective ways to spend your time. These 'pit stops' on the road to success should be used to re-energize and re-focus the client before they embark on the following month or phase of their training with enthusiasm and vigour.

A common complaint among clients of personal trainers is that they feel their coaches should do a better job of providing guidance and support before and throughout their workouts. Because of this, it is far more likely that you will give up on your fitness programme if you don't know what you've accomplished thus far, why it's working out, and how to keep it going.

In order to reduce as much risk as possible and provide a customer with a clear picture of their progress, progress reviews are an excellent tool!

The primary goals of a progress review with a customer are to:

The client should know how far they have come (preferably as a percentage improvement or achievement so they can clearly understand and celebrate with their support network, as well as specific feedback from you on "in session" progress relating to effort, intensity, focus, technique and reflecting on their feelings of well-being).

You should make it clear to your client why this growth has occurred (basically what were their motivations; how focused, dedicated, and motivated they were in their efforts to achieve their goals and learn new skills and knowledge) and how this advancement has benefited them.

It's important to make sure the client appreciates the importance of repeating and rinsing out the things that worked for them. Get rid of the things that make it difficult for people to show up and/or stick around).

Keep the client informed about what their training plans for the next month will look like, and make sure they are on board with any modifications that you are making to help them.

Because barriers aren't addressed, they persist and quickly interfere with client attendance. So, when the client's initial enthusiasm begins to wane, it will become increasingly difficult for him or her to overcome those barriers. There are only two options for you and your client to stay on track: either your customer must remain extremely motivated and determined or you must continue to help them at an ever-increasing level.

When reviewing a patient's progress, what is done?

The following should happen during a progress review with a client:

After completing the client progress evaluation form, you will need to identify and attribute elements that contributed to or hampered the growth of your client(s).

With the help of the client, agree on actions and timelines.

Ensure that training plans and programmes are up-to-date

It's critical to keep tabs on your own and your customers' fitness development whether you want to achieve your own fitness objectives or help them reach theirs. It's now easier than ever to keep track of clients' development thanks to personal training software. Here, we'll go through the many forms of progress monitoring, the reasons why it's so critical, and how to track your personal training client's fitness improvement. The following are a few of the reasons why tracking your fitness progress is so critical:

Maintaining a close eye on your client's progress can assist keep them on track, and it can also be utilised as a motivating factor for both parties.

UNDERSTANDING THE CLIENT'S PERSONAL AND FINANCIAL CIRCUMSTANCES

Qualitative and quantitative data can be gathered. This means that the CFP® professional must explain to their client what qualitative and quantitative data they need in order to fulfil their engagement and work with them to achieve it.

There are a number of examples of qualitative or subjective information such as the Client's current health and life expectancy as well as the Client's family situation and values, attitudes and expectations.

Quantitative or objective information includes the Client's age, dependents, other professional advisors, income, expenses, cash flow, savings, assets, liabilities, available resources, liquidity, taxes, employee benefits, government benefits, insurance coverage, estate plans, education and retirement accounts and benefits, and capacity for risk.

•

MODULE-6

FINANCIAL PLANNING: SUMMARY

The financial planning professional and the client agree on the terms for assessing and reevaluating the client's circumstances, including their goals, risk profile, lifestyle, and other pertinent changes. A review of the client's position is conducted to assess progress toward achieving the goals of the financial planning suggestions, determine if the recommendations remain suitable, and confirm any adjustments mutually agreed upon.

There may be one or more strategies relevant to the current situation of the client that could reasonably meet the client's objectives, needs and priorities; financial planning recommendations are developed using these strategies; and the financial planning recommendations and supporting rationale are presented in a manner that allows for an informed decision.

It is easier to build your own finances and afford the items you desire if you manage your taxes correctly. It's also feasible to considerably increase your retirement savings by preparing for taxes when you construct a financial plan.

The influence of taxes on society and the economy can be assessed using a number of widely accepted metrics. These are the standards must be met: economic efficacy, competitiveness, administrative ease, adequateness, and fairness in the allocation of resources.

The creation of tax advantages for personal financial plans can be used as a means of promoting specific personal aims. Personal aspirations like as property ownership, retirement savings, and education and health finance are viewed in the United States, as well as in most developed nations, as a way to benefit both the individual and society.

It is common for tax incentives to be implemented in order to promote the achievement of specific objectives. Purchasing a home, for example, is often only possible through the additional expense of taking out a loan. Homeownership and financing become more accessible and desirable as a result of tax deductions for mortgage interest.

Some retirement savings plans, such as IRAs, 401(k)s, and 403bs (so named after the sections of the Internal Revenue Code that establish them), offer tax advantages to employees who contribute to them. Taxable income can be reduced by contributions to these programmes, but only up to a certain level. Saving outside of a tax-deferred account might also be a good strategy for retirement savings. In addition to college savings and health care expenses, there are a few tax-advantaged savings accounts.

A technique that allows you to make progress toward your goal and get a tax benefit should be used whenever possible. However, your objectives should not be defined by your enthusiasm for the tax benefit. Recognizing tax consequences should inform your decisions without defining your aims because they change the value of your alternatives.

The tax ramifications of unanticipated events like an inheritance, a gift, a lottery win, a loss due to a disaster or theft, or medical bills are not unheard of. Unusual occurrences (and as a result, unanticipated) can be confusing, unfamiliar, and expensive. Consult a professional if you're in that situation.

Having a clear picture of what you want out of life and how you intend to obtain it should be reflected in your financial planning. Tax benefits and drawbacks are important to keep in mind, but they shouldn't be the driving force behind your decisions. For example, you wouldn't buy a property with a mortgage just to claim a deduction on the mortgage interest. However, if you plan to buy a house, you can do so in the most tax-advantageous manner.

Tax status change: Throughout the period you've been working on your financial plan, there may have been changes in the country's tax rules or the amount of money you earn. This could put you in a higher or lower tax bracket, resulting in a greater or lower tax bill. You'll need to rethink your financial strategy in order to lower your tax burden if you find yourself in this situation. If you are now in the highest tax band, for example, it is sense to plan your taxes carefully in order to save as much money as possible and better prepare for your financial goals. Keep in mind that tax planning extends beyond section 80C of the Income Tax Act, and that it is critical to utilise the other sections as well if you want to save the most money on taxes.

Changing priorities: Priorities shift throughout time. A vacation every half-year is typical for people in their early 20s; they also spend a lot of money on their lifestyle. When you have children and a family to support, your spending habits and goals will alter. Additionally, you may have additional goals and responsibilities that aren't included in your current financial plan. In order to achieve these goals, the strategy may require new tactics and investments.

Risk Tolerance and Risk Appetite: As a result of your age, past experience, knowledge, and other factors, your risk appetite and risk tolerance level play a role in determining how much risk you are willing to take in your financial plan. A person's determinants may vary as he or she grows older. Young investors, for example, are more willing to take risks. This means that the riskier asset classes in your portfolio, such as equities or real estate, will dominate. Your risk tolerance may be reduced if you are nearing retirement, therefore your asset allocation may need to be re-evaluated. The asset mix for a certain goal will need to change to less volatile asset classes like debt and fixed income instruments if you are nearing that goal's realisation.

An yearly (or even bi-annual) evaluation of your financial situation will give you a better chance of reaching your financial goals since it will allow you to account for any changes in your personal or economic situation.

You can also use a review to evaluate your individual investments and decide whether or not they are worth maintaining. There's nothing wrong with checking the current status and potential of your portfolio's equities, such as stocks and equity mutual funds, on a regular basis. When an equity mutual fund is not performing as expected, or if its investing objective or style has changed, it may no longer be suitable for your investment goals. This is especially true for equity mutual fund schemes.

Procrastination is the antithesis of personal belief in the necessity of change. You must understand that simply making a budget is not enough. If you want to achieve your financial goals, it is vital that you do regular reviews.

FINANCIAL PLANNING MISUNDERSTANDINGS

1. **It is a One-time Exercise**: A common misconception is that financial planning is a one-time event. In order to meet the goals set forth in financial planning, the asset portfolio must be rebalanced or readjusted frequently.

2. **It is Only about Tax Planning**: Financial planning includes more than just tax planning. Investment, protection, and estate planning are all included in financial planning, as well as tax preparation.

3. **It is to be Done When One Reaches Retirement Age**: It's a common misconception that financial planning can only be done when you're nearing retirement. If you're wondering when to begin your financial planning, the answer is obvious: yesterday. Consequently, the sooner one begins making money, the sooner it should be done.

4. **It is meant Only for Very Rich or High Net Worth Individuals (HNI):** Another myth is that financial planning is only for the wealthy. It doesn't matter if you're wealthy or poor; financial planning can help you achieve your goals.

5. **It is Only about Investments**: In addition to investments, financial planning also includes insurance, tax planning, retirement plan and estate plan.

6. **Financial Planning Does not Need a Professional's Advice**: Financial Planning is a specialized job. It requires deep knowledge of the various investment options, regulatory guidelines, legal aspects, etc. This can be done only by a professional qualified financial planner.

7. **Financial Planning Advice is too costly**: Financial advisors do charge fees for their services, and that is true. Keep in mind that the value of this counsel far outweighs the small fee you'd pay for it.

CHANGING TAX LAW

A new 2021 Act that was signed into law by the President on August 13 of this year has, among other things, altered the Income-tax Act so that no future tax demands can be made on the basis of a revision to Section 9 of the Income-tax Act.

In the Senate, a study of the tax measure takes place.... A two-thirds majority in each house of Congress is required to override the president's veto of the tax bill; if this happens, the bill becomes law without the president's signature.

For married couples filing jointly, the standard deduction will rise to $25,100 from $12,550 for single filers in 2021. In 2021, the tax bands for income tax will rise to keep pace with inflation.

Planned tax increases for 2021

Because of inflation in 2021, the tax rates, the deductibility of some expenses, and the standard deduction will all rise. The way inflation is calculated in the tax code has changed since the Tax Cuts and Jobs Act was signed into law.

In other words, rather than relying on the traditional Consumer Price Index (CPI), tax reform now uses a "chained" CPI to measure inflation.

In other words, this new figure accounts for consumers' desire to avoid things that see a high price increase by measuring inflation in a different, typically slower manner. Because of increases in the cost of living and/or annual raises that exceed the chained CPI, taxpayers may be more readily pushed into a higher marginal tax band than they were before tax reform.

Deductions and credits phase-out adjustments

Many tax deductions and tax credits will be phased out as a result of inflation adjustments, in accordance with these changes. Here are a few things to keep in mind as the phaseout process progresses:

In 2021, the maximum earned income tax credit for married couples with three or more qualifying dependents is $6,728; the credit is completely phased out at adjusted gross income of $57,414 for married couples (AGI). There is a maximum credit of $1,502 available to single filers with no dependents if your AGI begins at $11,610.

It is called the AMT: In 2021, there will be more exemptions and income phaseouts.

Individual Retirement Accounts: There will be no change in contribution amounts in 2021; nevertheless, the phaseout levels for taking deductions for these contributions will increase.

Individual retirement account (IRA) contributions will be phased out at AGIs of $66,000 to $76,000 for single and head of household filers, and $105,000 to $125,000 for joint returns, for active participants in employer retirement plans.

For married couples filing joint returns, the phaseout ranges from $198,000 to $208,000 for those with IRAs who do not actively enrol in another plan but whose spouse does. An yearly cost of living adjustment is not applied to the phase-out range for married individuals filing separately.

If neither the taxpayer nor the spouse participates in a job retirement plan, phase outs do not apply.

Planned changes to the alternative minimum tax

This is why the AMT was enacted: to deter the rich from abusing numerous tax perks and deductions in order to avoid paying their fair share of taxes.

A growing proportion of middle-income taxpayers were slapped with the AMT because the AMT exemptions did not automatically update for inflation until a permanent, annual update was put in place beginning in 2013. As a result, many taxpayers are able to escape the AMT because the exemption level automatically changes with inflation.

At $518,400 ($113,400 for married couples filing jointly) and $1,036,800, the exemption began to phase down at $72,900 and $72,900, respectively.

If you and your spouse are filing joint returns, you'll have to pay an additional $110,000 in taxes in 2021, or $73,600 if you and your spouse are single.

Changes to retirement plan distributions

It's important for taxpayers to know that those affected by COVID-19 were able to withdraw up to $100,000 from their retirement accounts without being penalized by the usual 10% early withdrawal penalty. Retirees' RMD requirements were also reduced by the legislation, which was signed into law in December.

This waiver of penalties and the easing of RMD requirements expires at the end of 2020 unless Congress passes new legislation.

CARES Act provisions that expired in 2020

Financial assistance was granted for a brief period of time through the CARES Act. Several clauses were extended, but others will expire by the end of 2020.

As a consequence of COVID-19's financial crash, this bill gave jobless aid to millions of workers. For those who are unemployed, the CARES Act established two additional initiatives to help those who are affected.

Worker's compensation for those who are self-employed or freelance, such as those in the gig economy, was provided through a programme called Pandemic Unemployment Assistance (PUA).

Unemployment compensation granted through standard state programmes were increased from 26 to 39 weeks under a second scheme, known as the Pandemic Emergency Unemployment Compensation programme.

Programs that have already expired but were listed in the law were extended for at least another year with the enactment of the Consolidated Appropriations Act in 2020. Employees will be exempt from paying taxes on their employer's student loan repayments until the end of 2021. First, the CARES Act prohibited evictions, halted student loan payments, and granted paid sick leave to low-income families.

ECONOMIC CIRCUMSTANCES IN FINANCIAL PLANNING

Economic conditions relate to the current situation of the economy in a particular country or area. As the economy expands and contracts, so do these conditions, which are influenced by the cycles of the economy.

Planning for the possibility that economic conditions will have an impact on financial realities is an essential part of financial planning. The return on labour (wages) may fall or it may be more difficult to expect a rise in income during a recession. Investing in new revenue streams can provide as a safety net in the event of salary reductions.

Analysis of decisions is at the root of economic theory. It's all about figuring out how to make money off of something by taking advantage of it. Financial and commercial decisions are heavily influenced by the macroeconomic situation and concerns about efficiency in the face of competition.

FACTORS THAT INFLUENCE FINANCIAL PLANNING

The country's economic growth: Economic cycles occur in all countries.

This signifies that a country's growth will be rapid for a brief time before slowing down. When a country is growing at a healthy pace, businesses thrive. Consequently, stock market values grow. In contrast, interest rates and inflation are still at historically low levels. During a downturn, a country's stock prices fall and interest rates and inflation rise.

Political issues: When a country has a stable government, the economy grows. Growth and social issues are vital, but certain political parties place more emphasis on the former, while others place more emphasis on social issues. As a result, the performance of stocks and other financial instruments is influenced by the political party in power.

Interest rates: Businesses borrow and lend money to banks and other lending organisations at interest rates. Interest rates tend to rise when firms want to borrow more money in order to expand their operations. Inflation is another element that influences interest rates. The Reserve Bank of India (RBI) may raise interest rates if inflation is too high. In addition to interest rates, there are a number of other factors that can influence them.

Inflation: Consumer prices are rising as a result of inflation. A company's stock value is likely to drop when inflation and interest rates are high because of the lower earnings. It's not uncommon for the contrary to be true, as well.

Our long-term aspirations are affected by inflation as well. The cost of the aim in the far future will rise if inflation is strong, so we must plan properly.

Global issues:

Many global challenges have an impact on our economy. We'll have to pay more for gas if the price of oil goes up over the world. Inflation is pushed upward as a result, both directly and indirectly.

Investing in India has a direct impact on countries that are undergoing economic troubles elsewhere, as do investments from India to the rest of the world. Our stock markets are affected by the health of the global economy, which in turn affects our economic well-being.

RECOMMENDATION TO ACCOMMODATE FINANCIAL PLANNING SITUATIONS

Typically, a financial plan is meant to help you achieve your investing goals within the time frame you have set for yourself. As a result, common wisdom is that it's best to avoid consulting your financial plan too frequently.

This is because looking at it too often tempts you to fiddle with your investments, which can jeopardize your financial goals. As much as this is true, there are times when it becomes absolutely necessary to review your financial plan.

Number 1: Change in income level:

Salary hike is an annual event, and it is usually taken into account while making a financial plan. So, it is natural to review your financial plan once every year when the salary increment happens and make some minor tweaks in your investments.

But there are other major events like – promotion, change of job, job loss, long sabbatical, early retirement, etc. when the proportion of your income might change quite drastically. Under such circumstances, your financial plan would need a close review.

As much as you need to ramp up your investments in case of a promotion or salary hike due to job change, you might need to scale down your investments during difficult times.

For example, in case of early retirement, if it is a planned one then, your finances are already sorted out.

But there are times when early retirement is not planned, like when there is a health concern or a family emergency, etc. During such a situation, you need to review all your assets and work out a plan to achieve the financial goals and also fend for yourself during the retirement years.

#Number 2: Occurrence of a milestone life event:

Some of the milestones events in a person's life are marriage, the birth of a child, buying a house, retirement, etc. During such events, as our priorities change to some extent, one may want to review his/her financial plan to add more financial goals.

For example, once you get married, you need to set goals like buying a house or a new car. As much as it was reasonable to be living in rented accommodation or commute by a two-wheeler when you were single, the same is not practical after you get married.

Meanwhile, when a child is born, you have to include financial goals like his/her education and marriage in your financial plan.

#Number 3: Opting for a big loan

One instance where it is an absolute necessity to review the financial plan is when someone is opting for a loan for a big purchase like a home or a property. You need to review your portfolio before applying for a loan and also after the EMI starts.

Now, before applying for a loan you should look at your assets to assess how much you would like to put down as the down payment. Meanwhile, as the EMI starts, you should once again review your financial plan to understand how much you can invest for other goals since your expenses would be increasing because of the housing loan.

#Number 4: Diagnosed with a life-threatening disease

Life is uncertain and evens the most careful and healthiest people can be diagnosed with the deadliest disease. For example, for cancer or multiple sclerosis, nobody knows the cause or how these diseases can be prevented.

Now the treatment of these diseases is expensive. Also being diagnosed with such a disease might require the individual to change his/her lifestyle that may include scaling down on working hours. This might lead to loss of income or less income.

During such times, it is essential to review your financial plan to alter a few investment goals. For example, let's suppose you have been saving for a foreign trip, but considering your health condition you might currently stop saving towards that goal and use the same money to create an emergency fund for treatment.

Also, less income means you might have to scale down on some investments.

•

REFERENCES

1. Financial Planning: A Ready Reckoner Second Edition by Madhu Sinha
2. Financial Planning Handbook by C.E. Scott Brewster, Lulu.Com
3. Financial Planning & Wealth Management Concepts and Practice By Joydeep Sen
4. 5 W's of Financial Planning: Master the Art of Personal Finance Strategy By Dr Vimal Krishna Rajput
5. Personal Financial Planning BY Dr Pradip Kumar Siitnha, & Dr Ajit S Thite, Publisher: Nirali Prakashan
6. Personal Finance and Planning By Dr Rajni

www.ingramcontent.com/pod-product-compliance
Ingram Content Group UK Ltd.
Pitfield, Milton Keynes, MK11 3LW, UK
UKHW021923190726
13853UKWH00002B/803

9 789393 239709